Sandown Baptist
Church.
Isle of White.
Sunday 2nd May 1993.

FROM PRISON TO PULPIT

FROM PRISON TO PULPIT

VIC JACKOPSON

MarshallPickering
An Imprint of HarperCollins*Publishers*

Marshall Pickering is an Imprint of
HarperCollins*Religious*
Part of HarperCollins*Publishers*
77–85 Fulham Palace Road,
Hammersmith, London W6 8JB

First published in Great Britain
in 1981 by Marshall Morgan & Scott
(now Marshall Pickering)
5 7 9 10 8 6 4

A catalogue record for this book is
available from the British Library

ISBN 0 551 00916 0

Set in Plantin

Printed in Great Britain by
HarperCollinsManufacturing Glasgow

to Sue
my dear wife
and best friend

Contents

Dear Dad,

I grew up. In fact I'm four years older now than you were when you died and left me. Did you know you were dying when they took me off to the evacuation nursery at Christchurch? No, I don't suppose you did. They tell me you were an optimist. I guess you had to be to have survived so long.

Your dad, my grandfather, was a boilerman on the TITANIC. *He left you orphaned when you were six, so you can understand how it was for us because you went through it yourself. How old were you when you became a bell boy for Cunard? Twelve? Thirteen? Gosh. I bet that wasn't all plain sailing. I've heard enough from old sailors to know that conditions were pretty appalling for ratings. What on earth made you go to sea when your own father had gone down with the 'unsinkable' to an icy grave? I suppose it was a job. They tell me you were a good seaman. Do you remember Paddy White who served with you on the* ATLANTIS? *He says you were a born leader – always involved in some scheme, he recalls, to put your name in lights.*

You made it in 1931 when you became world champion marathon dancer in Madison Square Garden, New York. Queeny, your sister, who incidentally still runs the Robbie Burns pub by the Old Dock Gate, tells me you lived in the States for some time making films with the likes of James Cagney and Fred Astaire. Boy, you really hit the big time until the squalor of those early years and 'horse killing' dance halls caught up with you. When you returned to Southampton to open the Peter Pan night club in East Street the tuberculosis had already begun its deathly work. By the time Hitler invaded Czechoslovakia you were unfit for active service. When he bombed your night club you moved to Malvern to open a café for the troops. That's where I came in. Do you remember 20th July, 1941? You even named me Victor to show your optimism and Malvern to remind me that those seven hills are a place of peace.

Your cough and your temper were now getting the better of you. Eddy, five years my senior, remembers your change of mood. Do you recall the occasion when you took all his lead soldiers and farm animals away from him? For years he hated you for that, until one day Mum told him how you had handed the melted lead in as our family contribution to the war effort.

In January 1942 you returned with Michael, who was then two and a half, and myself, still a baby in arms, to our home in Richmond Road so that you could become a security policeman at the Southampton Airport. Harry, my stepbrother, and Eddy, the eldest Jackopson, stayed behind in Malvern. You cannot have known then how permanent this separation was. We never again lived under the same roof.

Nine months later Michael and I were evacuated to Christchurch. Mum was in a Berkshire hospital giving birth to your only daughter, Doreen. You must have been excited about that because I hear you went down to the Bridge Tavern for a drink before setting off to visit Mum in Reading. You never made it. You collapsed. You were taken to the General Hospital and so robbed of even a sight of your only daughter.

Do you remember as you lay in that ward seeing one of Queeny's friends? She didn't recognise you when you called her over. That very afternoon she visited your sister and told her how a strange man had beckoned to her. Queeny told her off and said, 'The poor sod was probably lonely and needed a visit.' Later that night the friend returned to the hospital and discovered that you were already dead and that your name was Jackopson. She hurried round to Queeny, but too late to change your lonely death. Guy Fawkes night 1942, a five-day-old daughter and four sons became, like you, fatherless.

By the end of the war I had moved home eight times. From Malvern to Southampton, to Christchurch, Lyme Regis, East Wellow, Chetnole, Newbury and back to Wellow. After a short stay in the Home for Waifs and Strays I was admitted to my more permanent residence at Hollybrook Homes in Southampton.

Mum was apparently poverty stricken arguing

with one authority after another that she couldn't afford to have your three boys back. Eddy lived with your in-laws at Sir George's Road. Michael and I lived at Hollybrook, whilst Harry and Doreen stayed with Mum. I can tell you Dad, I was bitter. I was eight years old before I even knew she was alive. I had a card on my birthday just signed 'Love Mum'. At first I thought it was somebody's cruel joke until the housemother assured me that she was very much alive. That day I got angry with you for dying. I know that sounds daft but when you are eight the world looks different.

People wouldn't talk to me about you. I suppose they thought they would hurt my feelings or perhaps they just didn't think I needed to know. The only one who told me anything was Eddy. I used to visit him at Gran's house when I was about twelve or thirteen. He had a large sheet of plywood with all your old press cuttings pasted to it. You were my hero. Marathon dancer, movie maker, night club owner and entrepreneur. Once, a child care officer tried to redress the balance by saying that you were a nobody – but I knew better. You were my dad and even if I never knew you I wasn't going to have anyone belittle you.

Growing up in an orphanage wasn't all fun but I guess compared to your childhood I had it reasonably easy. In 1948 the welfare state was established so new rules and regulations made life at least tolerable, but I sometimes wonder what it would have been like living with you. What would I have turned out like with you as a dad? I don't

know and I never will but for what it's worth, thanks for being a part of bringing me into the world. Like you I'm an optimist and so far a survivor. They tell me that of all your children I'm the most like you. Anyway, without you this autobiography would not be possible. So thanks for the life you gave me.
Love Vic

1: Orphanage Boy

'Hey Jake – Catch.'

'Ta! Are you sure this stuff won't fry me?', I jibed, as I plastered another layer of olive oil over my sunburned body. I lay back on the grass.

'What a summer,' I thought, as I listened to yet another mud fight going on along the banks of the Test. The Wibbies had become our patch.

'Watcha doin' t'morra?' called out Larry as he swung out over the water on a rope in mock imitation of Tarzan.

Splash! He rose from the cool water with a splutter and a loud yelp and looked over to where I lay. Before I could answer, a muddy pair of hands dragged him down yet again into the water.

'It's your birthday isn't it?', quizzed Pogo, who was sitting behind me.

'Must be a booze up then,' mumbled another prostrated face down beside me.

Larry came dripping up the embankment and snorted his approval into his scruffy towel.

'It's your round Jake. Birfday boy buys the booze.'

'And no rum ya thick 'ead. Last time we 'ad to carry ya,' mumbled the leathery-brown body beside me.

'You're a fine one to talk,' said Jean, as she ran her fingers down his oily back. 'You was as sick as a dog yourself last night.'

Last night it had been my back she had paid such loving attention to but now it didn't matter. The idea of a party gave me a secret excitement which made even her sensuous fingers seem like sandpaper. Mates these were, but they would never understand what it would mean to me to have my very own birthday party.

'Got myself, a cryin' walkin' sleepin' talkin' livin' doll. Gonna do me best to please her just cos she's a livin'' 'crooned Pogo, wiggling his hips to emulate his hero Cliff Richard.

As he sang I mused. Birthdays had been times of acute loneliness as they seemed to highlight my isolation from a family which had splintered in many directions.

What had happened to my mother when her second husband, my father, had died I did not know. It seemed no one thought it important enough to tell me. If I had met her I would not have known her. Her world was not my world. My world was coloured more by the loss of Nurse Brown. Who she was I shall never know, but her passing out of my life was a wound carried through childhood more consciously than any grief over dead or missing parents.

It was Nurse Brown who had escorted me at the close of the war to Hollybrook Home for orphaned children. Not a word was spoken that morning.

We had spent the night in a farmhouse – where, I cannot tell. Using a tall white enamel jug she filled the radiator of the car. As I stood watching her strong, almost masculine arms bring the bonnet crashing down, she looked into my face and as quickly turned again to pat the car, as if to tell it something important was happening. Suddenly, from behind, an angry old goose came squawking after my legs. Brown kicked out to protect me and with hands like eagle's pinions she picked me up into her strong arms and held me close to her face. I had once been so afraid of that face that I locked myself in the lavatory to get away from her.

'I shan't come out,' I screamed.

'If you don't, I'll come in and get you,' she retorted. 'And when I get you, you know what to expect.'

I knew just what to expect. If I stayed in she would whip me. If I opened the door she would whip me. The bolt which shot so easily as I slammed the door of my refuge now seemed two feet above my head and I raised on tiptoe to open it.

'Come here you little vagabond,' she said in a voice like a magnet which drew me out of my self-imposed dungeon into her firm arms. She tousled my blond hair and put her face to mine and once again I breathed.

Now I was in those same arms again, rescued and secure, my short legs dangling out of the reach of a bad-tempered goose.

We drove all morning. A rare treat. Suddenly, we turned right into a drive hedged either side with mauve rhododendrons in full bloom. Brown squeezed my hand but said nothing. The car swung again to the right revealing at the end of the drive a huge white house. We entered the house by the front door. The entrance hall sported one piece of furniture, a dark oak bench seat with a high back. Brown lifted me on to the seat, put one finger to her lips and quietly turned to disappear into what I later discovered to be the office. Her business finished, we left the white house behind us. We walked up a black asphalt path towards several pairs of red brick houses. An enormous black shire-horse ploughed a field to our left. Eventually, we reached the house furthest away. We were met by a woman who ushered me into a room.

'Play quietly,' she ordered.

I went to the window to look at the ducks we had passed on the way across the lawn. Minutes later I saw Nurse Brown leaving the house. I ran for the door but was met by the woman who ordered me back into the brown and green room.

'I want Nurse Brown. I want Nurse Brown,' I shouted.

By now I sensed that there was something wrong. I dashed to the window and pounded my small hands on the frame. I felt hot tears on my cheek as I screamed for Nurse Brown to come back for me. Unkind hands restrained me but I broke loose and ran again for the door.

'Pull yourself together! Come to the window and wave goodbye properly. What would Nurse Brown say if she saw your temper?'

I was dragged back to the window. By now Brown was walking past the other houses towards the black path. She turned, waved, and resumed her steady step back to the white house and out of my life.

That night I lay awake long after bed time stifling each sob as it welled up in me. The lamplighter leaned his bicycle against the wall whilst he lit the street lamp with one deft flick with his eight foot pole. Soon the night was alight with the beams of searchlights playing against the blackness.

I fell into a sleep which as far as my conscious memory is concerned may as well have lasted two or three years. The events of that day swamped all other events.

My eighth birthday would have been as uneventful as any other if it hadn't been for just one card. It was signed 'Love Mum'. I could not imagine that my Welsh housemother had softened to this extent. She was Mum to her own two but not to those in her charge. My friendship with her youngest son singled me out for even harsher punishments as though to prove no favouritism. When half the day had passed, I summoned the courage to ask her.

'Your mother sent you the card,' she answered, as if it were the most natural state of affairs for a boy of eight to realise that mothers really could not be expected to do more than send the occasional birthday card.

I ran from the house down the black path to the copse behind the white house, an area out of bounds to all children. There, in the solitude of my very own beech tree, I cried. What does she look like? Where does she live? Will she come for me? On Saturday I would find out. Granny Glasspool would know.

Sir George's Road was my Saturday escape from Hollybrook. There I would see my elder brother Eddie. Perhaps he would know.

'Go down to the off-licence luv,' smiled Gran from her fireside chair. 'Tell her a shilling each way, and get yourself some sweets with your ration.' I clutched her bet and my pocket money and determined that before lunch I would ask her.

'Go down to the chippy and get some cod and the usual,' she said a few hours later.

My chance had gone. I could not summon the courage. My mother was never mentioned by me and though I may have met her once in my childhood she remained faceless and silent.

'Come on Jake,' called Pogo as he ran for the river. 'Don't forget tomorrow's the big day.'

'Where ya gettin' the dough from?' yawned the sprawling figure at my side.

'Oh it'll turn up,' I said knowingly. 'It'll turn up.'

2: Light Fingers

Criminal activity is rarely, if ever, a chosen profession. A series of foolish acts and petty pilfering become a habit; a way of life. The first time I stole was, I believe, from Mrs Westcott's purse. It was only a few pence and earned me a cuff round the ear from her husband who, though he was called housefather, was in reality the orphanage handyman. A thick leather strap was conveniently buckled around his middle. It occasionally gave the appearance of holding his trousers up, but this was a ruse for the unsuspecting delinquent who soon learned its true purpose. My introduction to that belt had been before conscious memory was able clearly to define events. I never remember a time when bedwetting wasn't met with a nose rubbing in warm urinated sheets and a 'Come on my boy. Take your punishment like a man.' It never occurred to me to point out that men do not like to have their noses rubbed in their own urine or accept a lashing without protest.

Soon after my eighth birthday I was to taste that same strap for my first venture into the world of housebreaking which was to dominate my life for the next decade.

I had not intended to break into the little terraced cottage. I had gone to see my friend as an act of defiance against the rule that all children should stay within the grounds of Hollybrook after school. My friend and his parents were out. Afraid of being spotted by Mr Shillabear, the Governor, who lived directly across the road from where I stood, I went into the house. For some time I sat in the kitchen my heart thumping louder at every sound.

'I wonder what it's like upstairs,' I thought to myself. 'I bet that's where Bob keeps his crystal set.' By the time I reached the top of the stairs I felt as if I would surely be sick. 'Suppose someone's in bed,' I worried. Gingerly I pushed the first door . . . and there was a sight which made me almost choke with glee. A bed so unlike the cream painted cast iron bedsteads in my dormitory. I'm sure I had never heard of or seen a trampoline, but I knew just what to do with that bed. It beckoned me to jump up and down in such a way that had anyone interrupted they would have been sure to certify me as A1 crazy.

Out of breath I flopped onto the feather filled eiderdown. As I lay there I looked at the fascinating furniture. On the small dressing-table something caught my attention and curiosity. A ring and a necklace and a number of brooches. Little did I know as I shoved them nervously into my short grey trouser pockets that this was just the beginning.

That evening we sat up listening to our favourite programme on the wireless, *Dick*

21

Barton, Special Agent. 'Da da da da da dum – Will Dick manage to escape the gas chamber? Da da da da da dum.' The paradox of my after-school crime and evening hero worship of the saintly cop did not occur to me as the signature tune died away and the scramble upstairs for inspection began. I was not even conscious of the sparkling treasures still entangled in the junk of school-boy pockets as Mrs Westcott began the nightly inspection of hands, ears and clothing.

'What's this Victor?' her Welsh voice lilted in mock horror as she held my untidy trousers aloft. Once again I had been singled out for my inability to fold my clothes neatly enough for her tidy mind. Before the next predictable sarcasm could draw it's blushes, out of my pockets fell my hidden jewels. The wooden floor of the dormitory echoed to the sound of a small ring as it rolled under my bed. I diverted my eyes to the picture over the fireplace. Birds and flowers in such crazy profusion, which had caught my imagination because of their thousand hidden patterns and pictures, now became a refuge from the inquisitive glare of my accuser.

'Ouch!' I flinched as my ear was twisted by her strong fingers. I kept my eye on the picture. A boy darted under the bed to retrieve my ill-gotten loot.

'Caw! Look at this Miss. Must be worf a mint.'

Laughter circled round my head, now tortured by an even firmer grip. My eyes began to well up with fear, embarrassment and pain. I was frogmarched to the top of the stairs.

'Mr Westcott! What do you suppose this boy's been up to now?'

'Is it that Jackopson boy again?'

'Yes, but this time he's really stepped over the mark. I declare this boy will hang one day.'

Mr Westcott seemed in little mood to wait for that day. His son stopped playing his violin and came to witness the certain lashing.

'I'll beat it out of him if it's the last thing I do,' growled the housefather as he applied his cure-all remedy. 'And to make sure you learn your lesson well, you can clean the boiler in the morning, and bumper the floor, and wash every sock in the house and when you've finished that you can go to bed without listening to Dick Barton.'

As I completed my punishment the next day the door of the locker room opened slowly.

'Hard luck,' whispered the familiar friendly voice of Paul. 'My dad doesn't mean to be like that you know,' he said authentically. 'He just blows his top when he's tired. I think he likes you really.'

'He sure has a funny way of showing it,' I carped back caustically.

'If my Mum catches me in here with you she'll kill me,' he countered, to remind me of the personal risk he ran in violating the code which separated members of the family from boys in care. He would play in his parents' sitting room, we in the common games room, but now in the no-man's-land of the locker room two boys 'cocked a snoot' at authority and determined just to be friends.

Soon we were wrestling in carefree abandon and my first encounter with housebreaking and its consequences were lost in laughter.

3: Mum and Pops

Every Christmas the children of Hollybrook were scattered into the homes of seasonal 'aunties' and 'uncles' who would try to make the holiday enjoyable. In every case that I can remember, they succeeded.

Often these excursions into families resulted in some fortunate children being fostered and occasionally even adopted. I had longed for almost anybody to rescue me from Hollybrook. If it could happen to Oliver Twist, thought I, why didn't it happen to me? Was there no rich uncle? Why did none of these Christmas families want an extra son? By the age of eleven all hope was gone. Nobody wanted a secondary school boy! However, a month after I had started at Shirley Warren School a jovial postman and his wife invited me out for a day. To my surprise the days turned into weekends until some four months later I was told the best news of all my childhood. 'You are going to live with the Smeeths, Victor. Remember all you've learned from me and do try to be good,' cautioned Mrs Westcott who seemed genuinely pleased at my happiness.

I arrived at the Smeeths in late January and soon discovered the delights of being an only child.

Toasting bread over an open fire, my new dad told of his days in the War as a desert Rat. I could not imagine this gentle giant as a fighting man. I sat fascinated by his stories. My new mother was almost as diminutive as I. Her hollow cheeks and rasping cough told me she was no stranger herself to pain but her kindly eyes and country accent gave her a homeliness which to me was sheer beauty. As we sat at the table to eat our toast and drink our Ovaltine, sticking stamps into my new album, I was at last at home.

Spring brought with it new adventures. Outings in Pops' pre-war Morris to Lincoln, Woking and Swanage. 'Go on Dad. Overtake him. Wow! You're doing fifty miles an hour.' Hollybrook was sinking further and further to the back of my mind as I enjoyed the company of two people who were more than substitute parents. They were real friends whose company excited emotions previously unborn. Sawing logs and helping to dig the allotment patch were not chores or punishments, as they would have been in Hollybrook, but unlimited ecstasy with two people I loved.

When Christmas came around I needed no other uncle or auntie. I was still at 52 Chatsworth Road. Already Mum had spoken to me about adoption. 'Do you mind having your name changed to Smeeth,' she inquired one day as she made my bed. I almost choked with excitement even at the thought. At twelve I had no past. My brothers and sister were already scattered.

Doreen, who was only days old when my father died, was back with my mother as was Michael, who had been with me for a while in Hollybrook along with Terry, my half-brother, who was already fostered out to a coal merchant in Woolston. Eddy was still with my grandmother. 'I'd love to,' I said without even a second thought.

On Christmas Eve we went to a sports cycle shop at the top of Lances Hill where I was treated to a brand new bicycle.

Such happiness could not possibly last. Its duration was already unbelievably long. Life in Hollybrook had taught me not to expect too much or to hold on too long to anyone or anything. I began to doubt that the security of the Smeeths was anything but another passing phase especially when all mention of adoption ceased. I did not know then that the child care officer had informed my foster parents of my mother's unwillingness to sign the adoption papers. The Smeeths had preserved me from such potentially damaging information by saying nothing; but their silence left me uncomfortable. I felt confused and wondered if they had changed their minds about me. 'Perhaps they don't like me anymore,' I thought.

If only they could have seen the child care officer's report they would have known that my mother was never actually asked her opinion about the adoption. He presumed, or maybe hoped, that my mother might one day want me back, so he discouraged any further talk of adoption by saying she would not sign the papers.

What made me start stealing from the home of the two people I loved I will leave for the psychologists to debate. I remember well the first of many occasions. Mum Smeeth kept her well-worn handbag in the bottom of the kitchen cabinet. I waited until I could hear her cough from the bedroom above. Down into the bag I delved pocketing some of her Craven A cigarettes and a half crown from her purse. The old man who had come to live at the Smeeths was the first to suspect my light-fingered habits as eventually I began to steal from him too. One day he successfully laid a trap for me and rather delightedly exposed my misdemeanours to my sadly disillusioned foster parents. He insisted that it was a matter for the police to deal with so I was taken round the corner to receive a severe warning from the Station Sergeant who was an old friend of Pops.

By now, however, I was beginning to get the feel for housebreaking. I had developed an ability for writing what appeared to be authentic letters enabling me to play truant from the Merry Oak School. Often I would break into as many as two or three homes in one day. The police began searching for a fair-haired small boy on a green bicycle. They even visited the school but always it seemed on days when I was absent, supposedly attending the ear, nose and throat clinic for a minor hearing difficulty. Nobody at the school suspected me. I was, after all, well-liked by my teachers, who on the annual report could think of nothing more damaging to write than 'This boy could do much better if he were to be less of a class comedian.'

It was ironically the Smeeths who uncovered my daytime activities. I had been to the scouts that evening following a successful afternoon of housebreaking. As I sat on the kitchen table listening to the radio Mum Smeeth playfully snatched at a comb which was protruding from my pocket. As she pulled it out along with it came a bundle of notes.

'What's this?' she cried, startled at such a huge sum of money.

'Oh, I was minding that for Mr Tear the scout-master,' I answered, hoping that my quick witted reply would satisfy her now obvious suspicion.

'Get into the car dear,' said Pop as he clasped the money. 'We must take this back at once.'

As I heard the car pull away from the house I realised I had been caught red-handed. They would get to Thornhill and within ten to fifteen minutes would be back with Mr Tear and probably the police too.

I ran to the garage. Oliver Twist came back to mind as I slammed the door and pedalled away on my green bike towards London. I was six months away from my fourteenth birthday. Two years of happiness were now behind me. What would I find in London? How would I get to London? At Winchester I stopped at a house to ask for water and directions. The lady looked down at me. I was still small for my age. My short trousers and open necked shirt must have been a give away. 'Stay there' she ordered, as one obviously used to issuing commands to lesser mortals.

'Darling – Darling' I heard her call. 'There's a boy here. Wants to go to London he says.' Her voice dropped into a confidential whisper. I stood there freezing.

A telephone bell at the bottom of the stairs gave away the householders' intention as the receiver was lifted somewhere else in the house. I realised to my horror they were calling the police, so turned on my heels and sped off down the garden path to my bicycle. I rode on not knowing for some time where I was heading.

Eventually, tired and frozen, I arrived at a fork in the road: 'London 49 miles Basingstoke 3'. There on the grass verge was a telephone kiosk. I huddled into a corner of my frosted glass refuge and fell asleep.

'Hello. What do we 'ave 'ere?' said a deep but not unfriendly voice.

I opened my eyes. It was morning. Up there in contrast to the red paint and the steamed up glass of the kiosk was the dark blue helmet of a smiling policeman.

'We've been looking for you son. You must be Victor.'

As he carried me to his car I thought of the Smeeths and cried.

When I arrived back at Hollybrook I was surprised to find that I was not returned to the Westcotts at house number 11. 'You're going to stay here with me Victor,' said the familiar voice of Miss Holford. 'Nobody else will have you, so you had better get used to the idea quickly,' she bumbled.

I recognised a few of her children but more important, I remembered her. The spinster who knew more about children than a dozen mothers. Her laughter could turn the most sullen boy into a faceful of smiles. Outspoken and often outrageous. Here was an old friend and confidant.

I was back in house number 1 from where I had seen nurse Brown disappear exactly eight years ago. Now the Smeeths were gone too. Even the Westcotts didn't want me but at least Miss Holford was still there.

I soon settled back into life at Shirley Warren School and six months later was transferred for my final year to Hollybrook House on the Millbrook Estate. The Smeeths did not visit or contact me; they were rarely more than a second thought away. Only recently have I discovered that they were not permitted to see me. The fostering experiment had failed so my rightful owners had repossessed me as though I were a luxury not yet fully purchased.

4: Behind Bars

We left the Wibbies on our motor cycles and made for Paddy's house at Maybush.

'You stayin' here tonight Jake?' called Paddy's mother from the bedroom.

'Yea. If you'll let me,' I said as I admired my tan in the mirror.

'We're gonna have a bit of a party tomorrow. Is that OK?' I called as I remembered my promise to the lads.

I'll have to set to work immediately I thought as I panicked at the idea of getting enough booze to satisfy my insatiable desire to impress my fellow gang members. None of us were Al Capones. Motorbikes, flash clothes, jiving and the occasional fight with other gangs of Teddy Boys at the Royal Pier marked us out to respectable society as an undesirable element.

Though I had decided to get a job on the buses as a conductor now that I was of age, right at this moment I needed enough dough to buy a new drape jacket and a luminous shirt and plenty of drink for the party.

Stealing had become part of my life. I had at fifteen joined the Army Catering Corps in Aldershot as an Apprentice soldier with a view to twenty-two years service; but even there I had been found guilty of stealing Post Office Savings books which I used by forging signatures to defraud the Post Office. After only nine months service I was discharged and returned to Southampton. There I lived with a docker's family who had befriended me in my final year at school, but again I abused their trust by stealing. On my seventeenth birthday I was caught stealing food from the larder of the Montague Arms Hotel in Beaulieu where I worked as a trainee chef. Six months at a probation hostel in Reading had failed to correct my now increasing tendency towards a life of petty crime. In recent months I had become more and more prone to burgling homes – sometimes just for the fun of it, but never with malice. I had developed a technique of only ever stealing half the money I found and rarely ever stole goods.

As I made my way up to Burgess Road past the first house I had broken into as a child many years before, I gave not a second thought to all that had happened since. Past The Avenue traffic lights, my pockets bulging with money, I stopped at a house bordering the Common.

'Ideal,' I thought with the eye of an expert. Front door hidden by a high hedge, no houses at the rear and mature garden trees either side. Perfect.

I rang the door bell.

No answer.

I walked round the side.

'Good thing I'm still small,' I thought as I wriggled through the small window. Once in the house I moved quickly to the routine hiding places. I was never one for disturbing a home. No drawers pulled out; no mess; just a tidy methodical search for 'Ah . . . here it is.' The money was enough to satisfy me. A busy morning but well worth it and as an added bonus a beautiful camera. 'I'll sell this,' I thought. 'It must be worth a bomb.'

'You'll have to pop back this afternoon for a valuation on this son. My brother's the one who deals with cameras,' said the second-hand shark of Shirley Road.

Naively I returned to the shop at two p.m. to hear the verdict on my camera only to find that I had been set up.

'Hello Vic,' said the Inspector as he came in behind me. 'I didn't realise it was you. Now I can get some of my unsolved cases cleared up can't I,' he laughed as we walked along the High Street, towards the Police Station.

It was a fair cop and I knew Brown was not a bad sort. The big question would be how many 'jobs' I could remember. Some had never even been reported.

'They probably never realised you were in the house,' he quipped as I signed the statement which was bound to land me in prison.

The next day I faced a magistrate and was remanded in custody at Winchester Prison until appearing before the Quarter Sessions.

'Get your clothes off,' rasped a sour-faced warden as the small batch of prisoners assembled in the reception wing of the prison. I sat on my bed and listened to the unfamiliar noises of jangling keys, slamming doors and the heavy echo of vibrating metal as wardens trod the cat walks.

It was morning and the reality came crashing in on me as my door was flung open and a voice shouted in at my isolation – 'Slop out!' As I carried my galvanized pot and queued up behind a line of prisoners in uniform grey I could not help thinking of Mr Westcott and his degrading punishment for bedwetters. Here was the adult counterpart. The smell was the same and the dehumanising humiliation was just as unnecessary.

As a remand prisoner I was kept in my cell for twenty-three hours each day. Half an hour's exercise in the morning and another half hour in the afternoon gave the only real contact with other prisoners as we marched around a small square.

Occupational therapy was provided in the form of large canvas sheets which when stitched became mail bags. I wondered whether my mail bags would go to the Southampton Post Office and be handled by Pop Smeeth, so I sewed them with what was even recognised by the warden as unusual care and workmanship.

We were allowed four library books each week to occupy our minds but inevitably these were short lived with so many hours to fill.

One day as I sat on my bed wondering about my

future, which was sure to be Borstal, I looked over to the corner of my cell. On a ledge was a little Gideon Bible. I had seen it there many times before and remembered back to the days in Holly-brook when on Sunday afternoons we were visited by Mr and Mrs Benke. For years they had taught us choruses and once when I had been in trouble they had promised to pray for me until I was converted. I had laughed then – not really understanding what conversion was. Clearly they had a soft spot for me. Once every third month, no matter where I was, Scripture Union Key notes would come through the post. As it was the only mail I ever received and it always came in the same kind of envelope, I usually discarded it as irrelevant rubbish.

On this day, however, I was drawn to the Bible like a dog to a bone. I was bored and at the same time curious. 'So and so begat what's is name and he begat the other one, and the other one begat you know who, and he begat the one whose name I can't pronounce.' I didn't even know what a begat was. What a strange book I thought. 'Blessed are the peacemakers' I read and laughed at all the occasions when I had seen peacemakers try to stop fights at the Pier. They normally ended up anything but blessed. 'If somebody hits you on one cheek turn the other' I read. That seemed like a good prescription for going through life horizontal. I read of the death of Jesus and some-thing stirred in me. Was it a memory, or remorse, or perhaps conviction? I do not know. My tear ducts began to well up as I fell to my knees and prayed: 'God, if you are there, you've got ten days to change my life and if you 'aven't done it by then you've copped it.'

How long I spent on my knees I shall never know. I wept for all the people I had hurt. I was ashamed and had no one to tell but God. My childhood and youth were gone. Would the rest of my life also be wasted?

As I got up from my knees I longed to tell someone. I grasped hold of the bell lever and rang like mad for attention. 'Quiet' bellowed the warden as he peeked through the 'Judas hole'. 'What do you want?'

'I want to see a chaplain,' I blurted out not sure whether I had gone mad or not.

'What do you want to see a chaplain for?' came back the impatient reply.

'I don't know. I think I've just become a Christian,' I stammered, convinced now that he too would think I was mad.

'Oh, it's the Methodist you want mate,' he said with unhesitating conviction as though every prisoner made this same request at least twice a day.

The next day the chaplain called. I told him of my spiritual encounter as he sat on my bed, his hands held together firmly between his closed knees gently rocking backwards and forwards. He listened attentively to the end and pronounced his verdict.

'This has never happened to me before,' he

chirped like an excited schoolboy. 'I don't know quite what to do.'

I waited, sure that he would think of something. He did.

'I know what,' he said, 'I'll send you up the *Methodist Recorder* each week.'

I had never heard of the *Methodist Recorder* and wondered whether he would ever get permission to send a musical instrument to a cell. When, the following week, a religious newspaper arrived, I was bemused to say the least.

By November I had read most of the New Testament. Though there was still much to understand I began to believe that there was a God who cared about me. I wanted to know him. I wanted him to change me. I wanted the kind of life I was reading about. Brand new and clean!

5: A Second Chance or New Life

'You know you're on Borstal report and what that means don't you?' quizzed Lewry the Probation Officer.

'Yea. They wanna see if I'm fit enough for three years down the line, don't they?' On the surface cool, arrogant and callous. That'll fool him. I congratulated myself and stifled my real fear of more time in the lock-up.

'How would you feel about another try at a probation hostel?' he teased.

'You must be jokin'. You know as well as I do they don't give you another chance at that. It's three years at Portland for me with my record.'

'You mustn't be such a pessimist Victor,' argued my tormentor. 'I found a place in London which will take you for a year but you'll have to agree to it before I can mention it in court.'

I looked at the floor and thought back to my prison cell. I remembered my earlier successful six months' stay in a Reading probation hostel. I had conned them into reducing my sentence by unbelievably good behaviour. Even when I was challenged to the customary punch-up I had declined in an attempt to keep my sheet.clean.

The bully had not the sense to lay off. When eventually I agreed to the contest of fists in the latrines, I made sure everyone saw him take the first kick. When I left him bloody faced in the urinal with water hissing from the plumbing all over his crumpled body, I congratulated myself not only on an easy victory but that the house was astir with how fair I had been.

'It was a good clean fight, Sir. You'd a bin prad of 'im,' I overheard one inmate boast to the 'old soldier' warden.

Could I pull it again. Six months was a nightmare of good behaviour but a year . . .

I looked up at the probation officer. Why should he bother? I had decided not to tell him about my religious experience. He wouldn't understand, I reasoned. He'd be sure to think it was a con. I even wondered myself whether it was just a flash in the pan.

'What makes you think I would do any better in London than anywhere else?' I asked trying to sound casual and non-committal.

'I don't – but I'm giving you the choice. Take it or leave it.' He was playing my game. I was a dab hand at reverse psychology and could spot it a mile off. But why? Why should this bloke care so much that I go to MacGregor House?

'OK,' I snapped. 'Give it a whirl – 'e can only say no can't 'e.'

He smiled and sat back with the satisfied look of someone used to getting his own way.

As I stood in the court room listening to his

bargaining with the bench I recognised all the old jargon of previous reports:

Father died when he was a year old.
Mother deserted.
Family broken up.
Failed fostering experiment.
Above average intelligence.
One more try.
One more chance.

A sense of helplessness gripped me. They were planning my life. My future was in the nod of a head, a knowing glance and the decision of one man who knew no better than what somebody cared to write in the Borstal report.

'I'm going to sentence you to three years' – for a split second my muscles tightened as I jumped ahead of his words to 'Borstal training' – 'probation with a condition of residence at an approved probation hostel for a period of not more than one year. Do you understand young man that this court is being lenient with you . . .?' His words became lost to the inner ecstasy of suddenly realising that maybe the God I had met in prison was working for me.

As the train steamed towards London I stood in the corridor looking out at my unexpected freedom. Gordon Lewry seemed to understand my need for quiet and sat motionless in his non-smoker pretending to read the paper. I avoided his occasional glance and wondered what lay ahead of me. I would not let anyone know about my prison cell prayers. I would be a quiet Christian if only to preserve myself in an environment which I knew would be intolerant of such deviant behaviour as reading the Bible.

Once delivered to the less than tender mercies of MacGregor House, my escort withdrew. Years later I discovered that Gordon Lewry was not only a Christian but actually prayed about every person he took to court. Now his prayers and mine were about to be answered in a chain of events which even today cause me to stand back in awe and recognise as planned and executed by God.

Mr Pitkin was without doubt one of the ugliest men I have ever met. His chin disappeared somewhere between his lower lip and the base of his neck. His glaring eyes and coarse humourless appearance towering above me created nothing but abject fear. 'Keep clear of him,' I cautioned myself. He looked even more sadistic than my Hollybrook housefather.

Two days had gone by and so far I had managed to keep my nose clean. No one knew I was a Christian and I had no plans to tell anyone. Eighteen blokes all with similar backgrounds to my own convinced me that to say anything about Christianity would be sheer folly.

'The warden wants you in his office,' shouted Wilson across the packed dining hall. All eyes followed the direction of his pointing finger and rested on me with knowing looks.

'You're in for it now mate,' said one of the older inmates.

'Don't let him intimidate ya.'

'It's just his usual rollickin'. We've all 'ad it.'

Cat calls and dubious advice followed me as I ran the gauntlet between tables towards the door.

'What had I done wrong,' I wondered as I nervously knocked on the office door.

'In,' he rasped loud enough for all the house to hear.

I stood in front of his desk and waited for him to take his eyes off the papers in front of him.

'What's this I hear about you young man?' he said piercing me with a menacing glare. 'You're a Christian? Answer me!'

'How did you know, Sir,' I choked.

'I've had this letter from Winchester Prison. From the chaplain. Says you became a Christian.'

I didn't like the way he said Christian holding the letter aloft like some court room exhibit sufficient to condemn me to the lions.

'Is that right?' he bellowed.

'Yes, Sir'

'Oh is it.'

I wanted to run.

'Well that makes two of us doesn't it?'

I couldn't believe what I was hearing. This was a Christian. This ugly overgrown ape.

'Right now,' he threatened without lowering his voice or softening its tone, 'if you're going to let this load of heathens know in this God forsaken hole that you belong to Jesus, you're going to tell them, aren't you lad?'

'No, Sir,' I answered with a speed and courage which surprised me.

'What! Are you ashamed of Jesus after all he's done for you?'

Obviously in his eyes I was worse than scum. Given a simple choice between his displeasure and the risk of upsetting eighteen delinquents with the news that I was a Christian, I calculated that my chances would be better with the lions than the prophet.

'I'll tell the first bloke I see, Sir,' I stammered.

I spent a miserable day trying to find the words and the courage to articulate my by now dangerous faith in Jesus. By bedtime I had told no one.

The brute was sure to come to me before the end of the day and ask if I had told anyone.

I know what, I thought in a flash of inspiration, I'll show them I'm a Christian by kneeling down at my bedside to say my prayers. I looked around the room at my companions. Some were already in bed, others sat around in various stages of undress delaying the inevitable 'lights out' call.

I knelt down and pretended to look for something under my bed. When I delayed as long as I dared, I straightened up, put my hands together, bowed my head and closed my eyes and waited.

'Oi. What's 'is name? What's that new bloke up to? Oi. It's not as bad as all that mate,' shouted a voice across the dormitory.

Everyone laughed.

Somebody threw a pillow.

I kept my eyes closed.

'Come on ya burk. Get up. You'll give us a bad name doing things like that.' The voice was ominously near.

Without any more warning, the jibes turned to action. Someone, I don't know who, pounced on me. Then another. Then another, and pretty soon I was flat out on the polished lino floor with several bodies writhing on top of me. I began to gouge at whatever eyes were available to me in a bid to escape my tormentors. Eventually the sound of Pitkin's voice sent bodies scampering good humouredly to their beds.

The real test was yet to come. I had been in institutions long enough to know that sooner rather than later somebody would offer me a fight. I had grown up with this expectation with every move I had made. So much so that I had developed my own technique. As soon as my would-be assailant had got the word fight out I would, with one sharp right footer, kick my opponent into battle. This principle of do unto others first what you think they are going to do to you had proved itself a compensation for my lack of height.

The following morning I was down in the basement kitchen cooking breakfast. I had been made kitchen boy because I had spent nine months in the Army Catering Corps – as a boxer. As the noise of boots crashing down the wooden stairs gave way to whispered silence, I sensed that something was afoot. I looked round as casually as my nerves would allow to see the suave figure of Mel Richards in the doorway. His Brylcreemed hair combed to perfection matched his spotless handsome features. Though taller than me we were about evenly matched weight for weight.

He looped his thumbs into his trouser pockets and addressed me in a manner which would have done my hero, Elvis Presley, proud. With a contrived curling of the upper lip and a nonchalant lack of expression he called my bluff.

'Oi. Christian! What you gonna do if I clobber ya?'

I was just about to let my foot fly when I realised that he had said 'Christian'. I had lost the initiative. I had delayed too long. Anxious faces excited at the prospect of another fight peered into the kitchen waiting for my response.

'I'll tell you what Mel,' I heard myself saying as though I too were a spectator, 'you hit me and I'll turn the other cheek – once!'

He rushed at me and landed the first punch. I fell. Now there was no turning back. They had all heard my foolish terms.

I stood up. Gritted my teeth and threw out my jaw in defiance.

'Right, there it is,' I snarled pointing to my Kirk Douglas dimple, 'but you 'it it this time mate and I'll kill ya!'

He drew back his fist and moved towards me. Suddenly his clenched fist relaxed and opened to box the air.

'Oh, forget it Christian,' he retorted and walked out of the kitchen.

Church had never held much appeal for me. Christians were thought a load of old fuddie duddies. Always very respectable and completely lacking in humour. Whether I fully understood at this stage what was happening to me is open to doubt. I wanted to be a Christian but lacked any real understanding of the Gospel. I had experienced God in my prison cell but what did that mean? How could that change my life? In fact I was no different. My clothes still marked me out as a teddy boy. I was still confused. No longer fully one of the lads but not yet one with the church.

'Go along to Chatsworth on Sunday,' counselled Pitkin's diminutive wife. 'They've got lots of young people your own age there and some of the hostel boys already go and enjoy it.'

I checked with Mel who like many of my previous combatants had become an ally and even a friend.

'Listen to me old son,' he advised with an air of one experienced in the ways of the church, 'you come along with me and you'll be alright. I've got just the bird for you.'

With some excitement I spruced myself for church. I only had one suit of clothes but I was proud of it. I brushed my velvet collar and adjusted my shoulder pads. Combed in my DA and slipped on my suede shoes. When I arrived at church I couldn't believe my eyes. I stood motionless outside the impressive new building whilst my mates went noisily in. What a place, I mused as I entered the plush vestibule.

Someone shook my hand and said a rather doubtful good morning, no doubt recognising from my attire that I was one of the lads from the probation hostel, all of whom had now disappeared from view. I looked into the sanctuary at a sea of heads and hats. One lady turned around, looked me up and down and whispered something to her partner motioning in my direction. 'Blimey,' I thought, 'where's the Queen?'

I went upstairs to be alone but to my amazement found that I was in a gallery packed with young people. Before I had an opportunity to check the girls Mel had boasted of, the minister climbed the steps to the pulpit. He looked like a cross between a waiter and a vicar with his dog collar, morning coat with tails and pin-striped trousers.

I was impressed by the way he spoke. No high-faluting religious jargon from this man. A down-to-earth commoner with plenty of wit, an easy turn of phrase and uncanny knack of making the most spiritual concept ordinary enough to believe.

As we left church he stood at the exit shaking hands with a seemingly endless queue of smiling admirers. I became self-conscious and tried to get past two elderly ladies to avoid his handshake.

'Hello,' he said thrusting his hand in my pathway as though to hold me at gun point. 'What's your name?'

There was no escape. The eager crowd behind

me surging forward was held up for a moment by this enquiry.

'Vic,' I said choosing my name in preference to my nick-names.

'Where are you from Vic?' enquired the clerical penguin as I gave him a crushing handshake to prove my toughness.

'From the probation hostel,' I snapped.

'Oh that's nice,' he smiled.

'Might be for you mate. You don't have to live there,' I carped.

'Well how would you like to come round to my place later,' he invited with what seemed a genuine attempt at cracking my resistance.

'He's bent,' I thought cynically as I remembered my street associations and 'queer bashing'.

'Look I've got four daughters and they'd love to meet you.'

'Can't be all bad,' I registered as I recalled Mel's promise of birds galore. The guy must be straight if he doesn't mind his kids mixing with the likes of me.

When I later met Frank Goodwin, the man out of the pulpit, I found a genuine friend who made Christianity so plain and attractive that I never could get enough. He taught me about forgiveness and held out the incredible possibility of a brand new life.

'This is it,' I found myself saying to Mrs Pitkin. 'This is what that prison bit was all about. The minister put it all together for me. God loves blokes like me just as much as the respectable do-gooders. He wants to give me a break. I can really go straight.'

She smiled knowingly, straightening her hat, a sort of multi-coloured woollen tea cosy.

'God is going to use you my boy, you mark my words. One day God is going to use you.'

'I've asked if I can be baptised,' I said encouraged by her openness. 'Do you think the gov'ner will mind?'

'No. As long as you know what you're doing. You will be a marked man in this house if you go through with it though!'

Six weeks later I stood up to my middle in a sunken bath at the front of the church. Five hundred pairs of eyes including all eighteen boys from McGregor House watched as the minister asked, 'Do you believe in the Lord Jesus Christ as your own personal Saviour?'

'I do.'

'Do you promise in dependence upon his Holy Spirit to follow him all the days of your life?'

'I do.'

'And it is because you believe that you wish to be baptised?'

'Yes.'

'Then on your good confession of faith I baptise you in the name of the Father, the Son and the Holy' – swoosh! The waters folded over my head and I felt clean inside and fresh and alive and brand new.

'I am trusting Thee for power,' the congregation sang as I wiped the water from my eyes:

Thine can never fail,
Words which Thou Thyself shall give me,
Must prevail.

The prophetic song ringing in my ears, I looked up to my young friends in the gallery.

'If anyone wants to know more about becoming a Christian, come down to the front of the church during the singing of the last hymn,' I heard the preacher say.

Just as I am without one plea
but that Thy blood was shed for me
And that Thou bidst me come to Thee,
Oh, Lamb of God, I come.

Who should come running down the aisle but Mel Richards followed by five other McGregor boys.

When we arrived back at the hostel I was appointed leader of the Christian group. Not that I had any qualification above any one of them other than being first to be 'dunked' as we called it.

Getting a job was no easy matter with a short prison record and lodging at a probation hostel. As a stop-gap I worked in the accounts office of Pride and Clarkes the motorcycle giants of Brixton, but my real ambition was to be a wages clerk. I wanted a job where I could actually handle money to prove that what had happened in a Winchester prison cell and the subsequent months was real.

Before my conversion I had planned to get a job

where I could plan a robbery from the inside. Wages clerks, I reasoned, were able to collect thousands of pounds from the bank. This was long before security companies had cornered the market on conveying large sums of money. Now as a Christian I would use that very opportunity to prove that I could handle the money but not steal it.

After months of trailing round London from one personnel officer to another and one interview room to another I was ready to give up the idea.

'Have you ever been in trouble with the police,' they would ask, and so the interview would end.

Eventually I found a company which seemed to ask no questions and was prepared to take me on face value as a wages clerk. Sun-Pat Peanut factory employing hundreds of workers in Camberwell Green would be my proving ground. The first pay day went by but I was not seconded to make the bank trip. 'Easy. Easy as falling off a log,' I mused as the thousands of pounds were disgorged from the bags onto the table. What a great temptation. Soon I would be collecting. I would then prove the power of Christ.

A few days later the manager of the department shoved a form across my Kalamazoo pad, 'Fill that in by midday. It's just a bonding form we have for insurance purposes. OK?'

I froze. I didn't know what bonding was but I knew what it would ask.

Yes. Sure enough. There it was. 'Have you ever been in trouble with the police?' What should I do? If I said 'no', I'd prove nothing except that I'm prepared to tell a lie to prove my honesty. If I said 'yes', they would ask awkward questions, realise that I was living at a probation hostel and that would be the end of my job.

'What's this young man?' said the managing director pointing at the form in front of him. 'Says you've been in trouble with the police. Is that right?'

He sounded so posh. So in command. The huge mahogany desk between us was a gulf that spanned two different worlds.

'Yes, that's right Sir,' I whispered, suddenly feeling the shame flush up my face.

'Well what are you doing in my wages department?' he asked raising his voice to a new pitch.

His startled look gave me new confidence. 'Working,' I quipped.

'Well go and get your cards. You can't work here with all this money. What on earth did you do wrong?'

'I used to break into houses most of the time, Sir,' I replied enjoying the game a little more each time his eyes reached new dimensions. 'To tell you the truth; when I was in prison . . .'

'What! You've been in prison too!'

I kept a straight face and continued, 'When I was in prison I became a Christian, which probably makes me the most honest bloke you've got in your wages department. In fact, I only got the job to see if I could handle money and not steal it.'

'Well I admire your gall. And pray what do we do if you fail?' The incredulity had overwhelmed him. He sat motionless gripping the arms of his swivel chair so tightly that his knuckles turned quite white.

'I never thought of that,' I said with genuine surprise. The silence was sickening. He picked the form up again. Pretended to read it. Placed it carefully on his blotting pad. Repositioned it. Sank back in his chair and yawned. Then folding his hands in front of him regained enough composure to deliver his verdict.

'I'll tell you what,' he said emphasising the last word into an audible sigh, 'You come here tomorrow at nine o'clock with the names of five people prepared to stand surety for a thousand pounds each, and you can keep the job.

He had won. Without losing face, he had won. Where would I find five people dumb enough to put one thousand pounds on the line with my record? Not a hope.

That evening I called in to see my minister to tell him the bad news. He smiled. 'You just sit tight,' he said with an air of someone used to taking on the world and winning. 'Let me see what I can do.' I felt uncomfortable and afraid waiting for him to return from the telephone.

'You'd better not let me down boy-o,' he said with enough of a twinkle in his eye to let me know that he was enjoying himself. 'Take this to your boss in the morning.'

I shall never know what was in that envelope, except that when I stood again in front of the mahogany desk I stood as a man.

6: Directions

After ten months at McGregor House I faced an unknown future. Where would I go? Back to Southampton? To old friends? Old haunts? New trouble?

I had made new friends in London and had a job worth keeping. I was now collecting wages from Lloyds Bank and facing the excitement every week of not stealing it.

'How would you like to go and live with the Weekes?' my probation officer enquired.

The Weekes lived in Dulwich in a fine big old house which the young people from the church met in from time to time for Bible study. Alfred Weekes was an insurance broker. Small, thin, almost Victorian in his manner and not much later in dress. A kind but firm face lodged behind national health specs and underneath a huge Homburg hat. He was in essence my exact opposite. Self-disciplined. Organised. Thrifty. Respectable. Hard working and above all holy!

His wife Jennie, ten years his junior, made his excessive goodness tolerable by being much more down-to-earth. Though she tried hard to be like him she successfully managed to fail. Enough, at least, for me to say 'yes'.

Soon the contrast between our lifestyles was to clash and become the foundation for much that has lasted into my own home life. 'Be in by ten o'clock,' he suggested. Had he commanded I would surely have disobeyed. When I rose at seven in the morning he had already completed an hour's Bible study and prayer and a number of household chores such as cleaning out the fire-grate. When he went to the door to pay the milk-man he was always armed with a wad of victory tracts. 'Which one of these haven't you read,' he would say fumbling through the colourful titles.

Money had to be accounted for to the last penny. Prayer meetings for the Poona and Indian Village Mission. Bible studies, visiting preachers and evangelists . . . How my rough edges must have jarred with such a saint. I was still unpre-dictable. One moment aspiring to true spirituality and the next admitting miserable failure.

By now I was twenty. I had become a member of the church and was involved to some extent with the Young People's Fellowship even though I was much older than the majority.

'I want to help in the leadership of the YPF,' I confided one day to a senior member.

'What can you do?' he asked.

'Nothing much,' I said, 'Maybe I can teach them to box.'

'Oh, we don't want that kind of thing here. You'll have to ask the deacons if you want to do anything anyway,' he asserted. I was not sure what a deacon was. I thought it was something you burned on a hillside when trouble was coming, but I was wrong.

The deacons discussed my offer.

'We've been given to understand that certain parents would not like to have their children led by an ex convict.'

The verdict was devastating. I ran to the prayer chapel where on Saturday mornings I used to pray with other members for the following day's service. In the quietness I cried. My past would never leave me. How could I go on pretending that I was something different?

'All I ask God is that you save me from going back to the streets,' I sobbed in prayer.

Two weeks later a man by the name of John Pudney stopped me in the central aisle. 'Vic, I understand you want to work for the Lord,' he said.

'Yes. But they won't let me here.' I replied caustically, still feeling sorry for myself.

'Well, you be underneath the northside of Waterloo Bridge next Friday at eleven o'clock. I've got a job for you.'

It sounded pretty kinky to me so I asked him, 'What do you do there?'

'We serve soup to the old tramps and preach the gospel.'

On Friday night and into the early hours of Saturday morning I ladled soup into huge mugs for the dozens of dishevelled shuffling down-and-outs.

'Go and give 'em the gospel,' urged John with a slap on my back.

'Do what? You must be jokin',' I protested in horror. 'This London Embankment Mission is your show. I'm just a soup server.'

'Go and tell them about Jesus,' he said. All you have to do is pick one and give him your testimony.'

I looked along the line of broken men. 'That's where I was headed without Christ,' I thought to myself.

'Buckets, though small, stood out from the rest because of his unusual appearance. A bucket either side of his bent-over figure contained his worldly possessions. I approached him cautiously. 'Eh mate,' I blurted, 'I'm supposed to give you the gospel.'

'Yea. I know,' he says. 'I gets it every week.' He growled without looking up from the paving slab which held his attention.

'Well you know more than I do then,' I said, trying to sound cheerful. 'The fact of the matter is I don't really know where to start.'

He cocked his head sideways like an early morning blackbird, squinted up at me and rasped, 'That's it mate you're on ya way. I'm listening.'

It was as if the Arch Angel Gabriel had come down and through this dirty old tramp commissioned me to preach. From the Fagins kitchen behind me a record scratched out George Beverley Shea singing the 'Old Rugged Cross'. In that moment I knew what I wanted to do. As I began telling 'Buckets' about Christ I knew I would spend the rest of my life introducing people to the most precious gift on earth.

I returned to Croxted Road. Alfie was already up and in his study. 'I want to be a minister. I want to tell people about Christ. How do I start?' I shouted in excitement.

'You start,' he said calmly, 'by being quiet. Then after breakfast you can help me mix some concrete for the new garden path.'

I was flabbergasted. What kind of spiritual advice was that! I sulked my way into the garden and listened angrily to his pernickety instructions on how to mix concrete.

'Now be sure to mix the concrete and the sand in those proportions. Create a good deep crater and pour in the water just a little at a time. I'll be back out in a few minutes to see how you are doing.'

'I'll show the stupid old bat,' I snarled under my breath as I shovelled concrete and sand carelessly together.

'Two parts of this. One part of that. Just a little water. Silly old fool. I'll show him.' Angrily I took a bucket of water and poured it into a hastily prepared crater. The mixture wouldn't hold. The sides burst sending a slushy mess all over the patio, just in time for Alfie to come out and see the chaos.

It was the only time I ever saw him lose his temper.

'Fantastic!' I thought as he stormed into the

house. He's human after all. I laughed heartily at my triumph.

Five minutes later I learned a lesson I was never to forget. He came back to the garden and gently addressed me.

'Victor, you were wrong to ignore my instructions but I was even more wrong to lose my temper with you. Will you please forgive me?'

I said that I would and realised that he had been indoors to pray.

'One day God is going to use you Victor. I don't know how. I don't know where but he is going to use you. For the time being he has given me the responsibility of preparing you and I don't know how to do it.' We went indoors to pray together.

It was a friend of the Weekes family and member of the Chatsworth Baptist Church who introduced me to preaching. Andrew King had been a Baptist minister but was now working for Dr Barnado's Homes. As Bible Class teacher, he introduced me to the concept of studying for the purpose of telling others. One day he invited me to accompany him on a preaching engagement to a small London City Mission. I was allowed to lead the service up until the sermon which of course he preached. At the end of the evening he invited me to accompany him again in a fortnight.

'Next time Victor, you must do the preaching. I will lead the service.'

'What!' I said in astonishment. 'Me? Preach?'

'Yes. You have a gift for it. I can tell.'

When I arrived home I told Alfie of the surprise invitation.

'Good. You shall do it,' he responded.

'Where on earth do I start preparing a sermon?' I pleaded.

'On your knees,' he said with a smile.

I did not have to wait for the next day. I was so eager that I began immediately. Praying, searching, reading, trembling with excitement.

Two weeks later I had exhausted my subject; the ten lepers who were healed by Christ.

When we arrived at Whiteleaf Chapel, a small green hut behind a row of houses off the A22, I was in a state of sheer panic. Andrew King, one of the finest preachers known to me, led the service. He introduced me and then sat back with a knowing glance.

I was soon into my subject. Absorbed. Excited. The words came tumbling out and the congregation followed every gesture.

'Do you know the forgiveness of sins in your life?' I rasped in rhetorical enquiry.

An elderly gentleman sat slap bang in the centre of the first row of wooden chairs, no more than two feet from the front of the platform from which I preached. He stood up, fixed his eye on mine in an uncompromising stare and addressed me: 'How dare you come here young man and ask questions of that nature. We are all Christians here.'

I gasped in horror and waited for my tutor to

rescue me. Silence filled the sanctuary. I looked at the menacing face of my accuser.

'Sir,' I choked, 'this is the first sermon I have ever preached. I can assure you that I have done little else for the last fortnight but pray over what I should say. I believe what I am saying is from the Lord so I can only repeat the question. Do you know the forgiveness of sins in your life?'

He sat down heavily and fumbled with his walking stick. I preached on with a determination to get to the end of my first and most certainly last sermon,

As I stood at the door to bid the people good-night, a young lady coyly took hold of my hand. 'Ya know, up to the part when the old boy challenged you I wasn't really listening to what you had to say but when you asked that question again I realised that I didn't have forgiveness of my sin. Would you tell me how I could become a Christian?'

'Now you're hooked,' said Andrew with a warm smile.

Soon I was preaching on every occasion that I could find a pulpit. The open air coffee bars, embankments, hospital wards, churches and chapels. Yes, I was hooked for life. Telling people about Jesus became an obsession.

Three young men joined me. Ian King, my teacher's son and Ken and Derek Moore – Crispin. Together we became the Messengers. They in music, me in preaching. Eventually we discovered the joy of introducing young people to

Christ through a balance of rock music and biblical persuasion.

If all this sounds as if I had become a super-saint overnight then I am guilty of deception. The truth of the matter is that I still had personal problems to overcome. Friends were held loosely. I had never formed strong lasting relationships. I left the Weekes after an argument over a broken cup. I broke it.

I would have been homeless again had it not been for the Porters who as newly-weds opened their home to me. The church became my family. Patient yet impatient. Loving yet sometimes hurtful. Wanting to understand my unpredictable nature but failing. Yet there like a magnet drawing me to its bosom even when I wanted to get away. A real family!

7: Off to College or A Lost Bargain

During my two years with the Weekes in Croxted Road I had begun to realise, I think through Alfie, my lack of education. I was fearful of meeting people who could in conversation expose my ignorance of even the most mundane facts of general knowledge. Consequently I was often embarrassed by middle class young people whose educational advantage was so obviously superior to my own.

'What you need', said Alfie, 'is a start with English Language at "O" Level.'

'How?' I retorted with some bitterness.

'Go to night school. Do a correspondence course.'

'Not another one,' I complained as I recalled the correspondence course I had already started with Kenley Bible College to improve my knowledge of the Bible.

'You'll not do anything without it,' he cautioned.

I knew he was right. I enrolled at night school and Wolsey Hall, Oxford, which of all the correspondence courses sounded the most grand and appealed, I think secretly, to my ego. It's one of those strange paradoxes of nature, or at least a quirk in my own, that when forced to admit an error of judgment I invariably over-compensate by turning too violently in the other direction. The mastery of English became an obsession. For the first time in my life I really wanted to understand the meaning of words and ideas. To my surprise education was no longer a closed door. It was one that I had never tried before. Gradually it began to open as my mind absorbed not just new knowledge but new opportunities. My love affair with the English language caused me at first to flirt with danger in conversations. I found that I could hide my ignorance behind a barricade of words and at times could even score points over my intellectual superiors. As confidence in speech grew so the balance was restored a little towards a more responsible attitude to my first truly academic interest.

In 1964, when I was twenty-three, I had occasion to speak to Frank Goodwin, my minister and friend. I wanted his advice about establishing a permanent ministry among the drifters of London's West End. By then I had graduated from serving soup to tramps to what for me was the much more fulfilling role of preaching to what were then called Beatniks. My apparent success with teenage runaways, prostitutes and homosexuals led me to think seriously of opening a young peoples rescue home in the heart of Soho. I had already met with a group of four interested business men in the Liberal Club to discuss the financing of such a project.

'What do you think Pastor?' I pressed after explaining to him my vision.

'I think you should get an education,' he replied calmly.

I was furious. I had wanted him to endorse my scheme and by a one-sentence broadside he had almost shot me out of the water.

'What do you mean? Get an education! I don't need any of that "la de da" stuff. I see people converted on the streets and in the coffee bars every week. I preach every Sunday with the Messengers and dozens of people respond to my invitations to accept Christ. I don't need an education – all I need is backing.'

He smiled the smile of a benevolent father and I knew instinctively I had lost.

'Do you believe that Jesus died for everyone?' he quizzed.

'Of course I do,' I sulked.

'Then if you really believe that, you will get an education. God doesn't want you just to speak to drop-outs. You'll always be able to communicate with them because of your background. God wants you to be able to speak to others as well. You have a gift which needs cultivating for God.'

I sat silently looking at the floor. I knew he was right but didn't want to lose my own private ambition.

'Look, today's Tuesday,' he went on ignoring my pouts. 'On Friday there is a Ministerial Recognition Committee at Baptist Church House. I want you to come before it as the first stage of applying for Spurgeon's College.'

I knew of Spurgeon's College because Paul, one of our Young People's Fellowship, was a Beasley-Murray, son of the Principal.

'They'll never accept me at Spurgeon's,' I protested knowing that the College had a reputation for always turning down more people than it accepted.

On Friday I sheepishly found my way to the denominational headquarters in Holborn. By now I had struck a bargain with God which I knew was infallible. Knowing the high standard required and that I would need not only to pass an entrance examination but also to be recommended by my church, the Ministerial Recognition Board, and the College Council, I would go through the procedure with the sure and certain knowledge that I would never be accepted for training.

'I'll put myself forward for training,' I prayed, 'but if I am not accepted I will take it as a sign that you want me to carry on with my plans for a hostel in Soho.'

I waited nervously for my name to be called. The friendly face of Gordon Fitch appeared.

'Your turn Victor,' he said with a reassuring beam. 'When you get in you will find the men sitting in a semi-circle. You make your way to the one vacant chair at the end of the row on the right.'

I don't know why, but I had not expected to see my own minister in the Chairman's position at the front. It had never occurred to me that as

President of the Union for that year he should have such a position. I sat down next to a rather large, elderly gentleman. Somehow his spats did not seem out of place in this rather grand building which had obviously seen better days. He folded his hands across his oversized corporation, as if to protect his pocket watch, and looked to where I was seated at his right hand.

'And what makes you think yerrr called to the ministreee young man,' he rasped in a Scottish accent no doubt cultivated to put the fear of God into inferior wee Englishmen, 'and the Baptist ministre-e-e at that?'

I had been forewarned that the bark of Angus McMillan was worse than his bite or I may have chosen that moment to give up all thought of ministry.

'He does!' I said with a cheekiness that surprised even me as I pointed to the chair occupied by my minister. Even Angus laughed.

To my horror the committee recommended that I apply to Spurgeon's College.

'You will need to prepare for college', they said, 'by studying New Testament Greek, Baptist History and Baptist Doctrine.'

I was introduced to an Indian gentleman in Streatham who for five shillings an hour would teach me Greek. How does an Indian come to be teaching Greek, I wondered, as I sat in his dingy front room filled with strange smells. I am not sure whether it was he or I who failed in this noble attempt but when I eventually arrived at the

College to sit my entrance examination I was still painfully reciting, Alpha, Beta, Gamma, Delta and so on!

'Where have you been?' enquired a tutor upon my arrival at what seemed a very impressive country house set in its own grounds in the unlikely sprawling suburb of Upper Norwood. 'You're late', he pleaded as though I had injured him personally.

I was ushered into the lecture room where heads raised in astonished glances as I was shown to my desk. 'That's cooked it,' I thought as I put my head down to the paper to avoid the eyes of more studious applicants.

As I retraced my steps to the College a little later in the Spring I couldn't help wondering if my little bargain with God wasn't going somewhat awry. The Recognition Committee had given their approval to my application. My fellow church members had voted in favour of my being trained. The exam fiasco was my only hope to date. To this day I cannot remember why I should have thought the exam would start an hour later than every other student, but at least it made the score 2–1. Everything now hinged on the College Council. I was shown into a classroom adjoining the dining hall and asked to sit on a small platform next to a man whom I recognised as the Principal. A hundred eyes gazed up at me as one after another of my inquisitors fired questions all of which I was convinced were loaded to trap the unsuspecting.

'Perhaps you would tell us Victor what theological books you have read in the past year,' said one of the faces now lost in the oblivion of my memory.

'I started to read a book called *Baptism in the New Testament* by a man called Beasley-Murray,' I chirped, 'but it turned out to be a race between that and the Oxford English Dictionary. The dictionary won.'

The sober body of ministers broke out into spontaneous laughter, hoots and catcalls as the Principal stood to take a bow.

'And what makes you think you will be able to understand other books if you cannot come to grips with a simple introduction to baptism?' quizzed the author in a voice that was kindly and unthreatening.

'I presume, Sir, you will teach me that,' I said in a desperate attempt to control my innate love of being a comedian.

I was shown out of the room so that Council could debate my fate in private. It was not until many years later that I discovered how much the discussion revolved around my lack of academic achievement and poor results in the entrance examination. It was the founder of the college, long since dead, who won the day. C. H. Spurgeon had decreed that any man, regardless of educational disqualification, who had a genuine call of God to the ministry should be accepted by the College so that he may be better equipped to fulfil that ministry. And so I was accepted with my English language 'O' level. I would have to study during the first year for two more 'O' levels and two 'A' levels in order to be accepted by London University for a Bachelor of Divinity external course. I passed 'O' level in English literature and history, and at 'A' level in religious knowledge. The one examination I felt most confident over was to be my greatest disappointment.

The exam was to take place in Chelsea Town Hall at two p.m. I arrived at the hall at ten a.m. remembering my lateness at a previous exam. I sat on a bench revising my swat cards, congratulating myself on my promptness and preparation. At two p.m. I entered the hall with my registration card and searched for my desk. I could find no corresponding number. An invigilator seeing my predicament checked my card.

'This examination was this morning,' she said.

I stood numb.

Dazed, I travelled back to college. A year's work wasted. The new syllabus would mean starting back at square one.

I told Mr Fitzsimmonds, my tutor, of my disappointment.

'Oh Mr Jackopson,' he groaned, 'I don't know whether to console you or to shoot you.'

I could have willingly taken the latter. To sit the degree would mean a further year added on to the four year course. I was impatient. I wanted to get out into the real ministry.

It was perhaps one of the biggest mistakes of my life to have given up so easily. The college had the wisdom to leave the choice in my hands. I made the wrong decision. Whether out of self pity or impatience or plain laziness I chose to finish my final three years and leave without the satisfaction of a degree. The staff persevered and pumped as much useful information as they were able into what was clearly one of their less successful students.

My fellow students looked upon me with fluctuating endearment and exasperation. Not many petty criminals get into theological college. I believe in their eyes what I lacked in education I made up for in experience, especially on occasions when rivalry with other colleges required the gentle art of breaking-in to 'borrow' a mascot or two before a football match.

On one occasion Lord Coggan, then Archbishop of York, was to lecture for a week on the subject of 'Prayer in the New Testament'. David Coffey thought it would be a good idea to 'borrow' the magnificent portrait of the reverend gentleman from the London College of Divinity. In order to confuse the matter a little it was suggested that we should break into all four London theological colleges and transfer items of interest from one to the other under cover of darkness and sit back to watch the confusion the next day.

The first place of entry was to be London Bible College in the Marylebone Road. With a bunk up from David Coffey it was fairly easy to get in through a rear window. I tip-toed through the building looking for a prize possession to transfer. I stumbled over a desk; stopped to allow my eyes to become more accustomed to the dark . . . To my horror I saw rows of desks with typewriters on them and filing cabinets. I had not broken into the college but an adjoining block. 'If I get caught in here it's back to prison for me,' I thought, so without more ado I jumped out of the window to find another way into LBC.

The Archbishop never did find out who 'borrowed' his portrait to grace our lecture hall for the week.

College rags were not always confined to extra-mural activities. Childish pranks like popping a hedgehog into a classroom where a lecture was in progress or hiding alarm clocks set to go off at intervals during elocution lessons made the more serious task of study more tolerable.

Ironically I was awarded the senior prize for elocution. At the end of my course what I lacked in formal education was more than compensated for by the discovery of myself. I was at last a person with recognisable strengths and weaknesses. I began to understand the way I tick. My beliefs had been challenged. My faith had been tested. My mind had been opened to new truth without destroying the core of what I had. I had become, somewhat belatedly, at twenty-seven, a man.

'You'll never last the course,' Mary Hudson had said a few days prior to my entry – but for once she was wrong.

8: New Horizons

During my college course my eyes had been opened to wider issues of the Christian faith. Evangelism ran through every fibre of my being but thanks to Rex Mason I began to question matters of justice, morality and the complexity of world problems such as race and war. I had joined student demonstrators marching through London in the naive belief that banners could change politics.

It was, therefore, natural for me to accept the invitation of an inner London church to become their minister. Wandsworth had become a multi-racial society with many immigrant groups, especially from the West Indies. Juvenile delinquency was an aggravated sore in the community with skin heads and greasers constantly at war.

I had already chosen to study experimental youth work and race relations in the United States for an academic year, so the church agreed to ordain and induct me as their pastor in September 1968, but wait until the following July for me to take up my responsibilities.

It was in Switzerland that one of those strange ironies of fate, which some people call coincidence but others recognise as the hand of God, happened to influence my life profoundly. I was attending the Baptist World Youth Conference in Berne as a youth group leader. Some of the greatest Christian statesmen and speakers were there to challenge the thousands of teenagers to see the world as one vast mission field.

A radical element from a number of European countries clubbed together to protest that the conference was 'all talk and no action.' They threatened to completely disrupt the proceedings if their voice was not listened to. Strangely and inexplicably I was drawn into the middle of this debate to act as a mediator between the radical students and the organisers. The immediate outcome was a compromise which meant me putting to the conference a motion that a special offering to buy food for the poor be taken after Billy Graham's speech. This was agreed to the delight of students and organisers. The affair had, however, brought me into contact with a number of people from the United States, one of whom was a member of the Baptist Home Mission Board in Atlanta, working among students.

Ed Seabough had stood by me during the debate holding the middle ground as a peacemaker. We spent some hours in each other's company and became firm friends.

'I hope I may see you when I get to the States,' I said to him over lunch.

'What are you going to do in America?' he asked.

'Oh, I'm going to travel around to try and understand a little more about the ways in which you are coming to grips with such problems as race and juvenile delinquency in order that I can be a better minister. A business man in London has paid my fare and my college principal is trying to get someone to arrange things for me over there. The London Baptist Association are acting as official sponsors,' I replied, knowing full well that Dr Beasley-Murray had drawn a blank because his contact had not replied to his letter.

'What's your itinerary?' he asked. Now the cat was out of the bag. All I had was an air ticket to San Francisco.

'You had better let me take care of this,' said my new friend.

Within a few weeks I had an itinerary which was to take me from San Francisco to New York visiting nearly every major town in the USA in over half the states north, south, east and west. I was able to be the guest of the Southern and American Baptist Conventions, and see over two hundred projects among the poor in ghettos and young hippies on the streets of Haight Ashbury, Sunset Strip and Greenwich Village.

The next obstacle to overcome was that of getting a visa. The United States has understandably very strict entry regulations, one of which bars folk like myself who have had encounters on the wrong side of the law. I was refused. Even though my offence was by then almost a decade past I was politely informed that I was *persona non grata*.

Sir Cyril Black, the then member of parliament for Wimbledon, wrote to the Embassy appealing on my behalf and at the last moment a temporary visa was issued. With much excitement I said goodbye to the church members at Wandsworth who would wait patiently for ten months for my return. The following day I was in the sweltering heat of San Francisco.

Here I met a life style which made my mind boggle. Wealth and poverty cheek by jowl. A world of contrasts which made Alice in Wonderland seem the height of normality. As I walked along the Haight Ashbury a long haired hippie pressed a flower into my hand and wished me peace. A young man with a sandwich board which looked like a computer punch card walked towards me. He stopped so that I could read his message, 'Do not bend, fold or mutilate, I am a living person.' He smiled at my perplexity.

I entered a coffee bar called the 'Love Shop' and found it was a Christian rescue centre where ministers were indistinguishable from the drifters. I thought back to the previous summer which I spent living on Brighton Beach as a hippy ministering to the drop-outs – an oddity in England, but perfectly normal in San Francisco. I was taken to Huckleberry's House, a home for runaway boys, and thought back to my unrealised dream in London. Here it was a fact of life. Hundreds of teenagers gravitated to that one street from all over America. Here Christians were involved in liaising with parents and where possible reuniting families. Here was the living proof that where sin abounds there much more does grace abound. For a whole month I stayed at the Golden Gate Seminary studying, with the help of Francis Dubose, the amazing world of drop-out USA.

Ron Willis, a young Baptist minister, showed me the Berkely Campus where blue helmeted guards threw smoke bombs to disperse unruly student demonstrators who were complaining about the expulsion of Eldridge Cleaver the black political activist. We walked down to the court house where some hundreds of students had congregated to protest. As we waited wondering what would happen next a freckle-faced fiery street preacher stood on a wall and in a loud voice called down the wrath of heaven upon his involuntary congregation.

'God will judge you for your actions today,' he bellowed. 'Jesus never demonstrated or marched anywhere.'

'Didn't he?' I whispered to Ron. 'He demonstrated his love for us and marched all the way to the cross.'

I felt a tap on my shoulder.

'What's that you say, man?' Rasped a tall black man who had been standing behind me and overheard our conversation. 'You tell it like it is man. Get up there and tell us about Jesus. Hey gang. This guy is cool, let's hear it from him.'

Ron mounted the wall first and spoke until the freckled man tore his clerical collar off. There was nothing for it; I now had to get up and preach Christ to my strangest congregation.

The next day I visited San Quentin Prison. This was to be the first of many visits to different jails and penal institutions around the country. At home I belonged to the Howard League for Penal Reform but it was here in America that I finally became convinced of the evil influence of a prison system. Obviously dangerous criminals must be separated from society to protect the innocent, but when petty offenders are caged up in cells with evil men only greater harm can be done to the society. Even whipping or the stocks would be more humane than the violence of a dehumanising system where men become animals and learn the survival of the gutter.

From San Francisco I travelled south to Fresno where I spent a week in schools and conducted a daily three-hour phone-in on local radio to answer questions from teenagers. Fresno had become a prime outlet for the drug traffickers from San Francisco and Los Angeles, consequently many of the young people had problems related to the drug culture.

In Dallas I was to be the guest of the H. L. Hunt family. He was reported to be the richest man in the world so it was with some fear and a massive inferiority complex that I drove up to the impressive replica of Mount Vernon, the Washington home of George Washington. As I got out of the car his daughter June warned me of a current bomb threat which had been issued by black militants. 'Don't worry,' she reassured me, 'there are plenty of guards but you must make your way briskly from the car to the house.'

I wondered later what H. L. Hunt would have said if he learned that his younger daughter Swanie had accompanied me to an all black church on Sunday, and what the black congregation might have said had they known that his flesh and blood had entered their sanctuary. I recall that Sunday well. It was the first time I had preached in a 'black church'. The congregation were enthusiastic, even downright happy. I preached on the theme of deliverance. I'm not sure whether they heard me, for their vocal response throughout my sermon made it difficult for me to hear myself. However, when I reached the climax of my talk they gave a standing ovation. The minister cried out behind me, 'That's it baby, sock it to them, sock it to them.'

At the end of the service I was made to stand at the front of the church as each member filed by to give me a love offering.

In Atlanta I met black civil rights workers and civic leaders such as Ralph Abernathy and Julian Bond who impressed me with their integrity. There I attended the fortieth birthday celebration of Martin Luther King, who only months before had been shot in Memphis. His little Baptist Chapel was filled with family and friends still in mourning. I felt the heartbeat of the oppressed marching to victory as we marched arm in arm to a new housing project which had become a symbol of hope borne out of a leader's death.

When I moved on to Memphis I was to experience the full impact of racial prejudice. I was to preach on Sunday in the Bellevue Baptist Church. On the Wednesday afternoon the minister showed me into his sanctuary.

'I wan' you ta know young man,' he drawled, 'that when you preach at ma church you're preachin' in the second largest in the convention.'

I looked round in bewilderment. Wall to wall carpeting and a chandelier which would have looked at home in a French palace.

'When ya preach ya need ta have in mind that thousands will be watchin' ya on television. I have one ambition before I leave this church,' he went on, 'I want ta turn those cameras into colour.'

I smiled to myself at this display of immodesty which, contrary to popular opinion, is quite rare in the southern states. He ushered me out to the recreation building which sported a full gymnasium, skating rink and bowling alley.

'Boy, what I wouldn't give to have something like this in London,' I boggled, 'You must really be able to reach the kids around here.'

'This is not for them,' he boomed. 'This is for our church young people.'

It was then I realised that the church was surrounded by an all black ghetto.

When I got up in the pulpit to preach I was still smarting with something less than righteous indignation. I talked of how Baptists began in Europe at the beginning of the seventeenth century a persecuted minority. Of how some left the country they loved because they were not allowed to worship within five miles of a town or receive an education. Some became citizens of America and built little tin and wooden chapels. God blessed their faith and industry so they built bigger churches. Then they put in carpets, wall to wall, and chandeliers. It was then that I completely lost my cool. 'I wouldn't be sitting under that chandelier for all the tea in China,' I blasted pointing to the offensive lighting, 'for when God judges this church, it's not up there in the television cameras you need your colour, it's down here in the pews – black and white together.'

I have never experienced such an immediate response to a sermon. The excitement of the many students from the local university could not be contained. They ran down the aisles to the front of the church and hugged me, kissed me, shook my hand.

'Boy, we've waited years to hear that,' said one idealist.

'You had better get out of Memphis,' advised another.

'I suppose you realise that there will be no honorarium for you today,' said a cold voice behind me. 'You have abused our hospitality.'

I cannot tell twelve years later whether I would do the same again. I'm sure my words were those of a hot-headed idealist but I do believe that America and especially the Southern States have begun to change. It is significant that on a recent visit to that same church the only bodies found in the gymnasium were all black and that under the leadership of another minister the church has grown even more.

Later on in Chicago I was to taste the awful reality of reaction. Operation Breadbasket was a practical programme of self help for the city's Southside black community. I was invited to attend a Saturday morning rally at which the Rev Jessie Jackson would speak. Mine was the only white face in the audience. I was introduced from the platform as English and friendly, thankfully before the main speech of the rally.

'I wanna tell you my black brothers about this here meltin' pot we call the United States of America,' he commenced. 'As I look into this pot I see the stew all bubblin' and hot. Floating around on the top I see the green peas. Now that reminds me of the Irish. We got more of them in Chicago than they got in Ireland. Then I see the carrot which reminds me of the Jew. He's got more carrots than anybody else! Then I see the meat. The honky tonk. The WASP (White Anglo Saxon Protestant). He's got the best of the stew. But where are we? We are at the bottom of the melting pot. The last to be seen but the first to get burned.'

All pandemonium broke loose as men cheered and threw their fists into the air. I felt like a black man at a Klu Klux Klan planning session I kept my eye on the illuminated sign marked 'exit' as he brought his speech to a climax.

'I tell you my brothers, when we riot and burn down our own homes and shops we've got it all wrong. If we don't soon get our rights we are goin' to take this great big melting pot and turn it upside down so that we're no longer on the bottom.'

Now I felt was an appropriate time to leave. I had already been robbed on the street the previous day so had a natural instinct for self preservation.

In Nashville I was told again, 'Don't go out to the poor area at night' – so I decided to go during the day. Children played games in the street the same as anywhere in the world. As I walked along enjoying some of the most pleasant weather of the whole trip, a bunch of kids followed behind me. Men rarely walk even in the poor areas of America because society is geared to the automobile. Effective public transport is a fairly recent innovation even in many of the larger cities.

I heard the excited giggles of my uninvited followers. Suddenly I ducked down behind a fence and pretended to shoot at the posse of ten year olds. One fell flat and writhed in mock death throws whilst another lobbed an imaginary grenade. Moments later I was surrounded by a mob of young inquisitors who wanted to know everything from my origins to the chip on my front tooth.

'Come and meet my mother,' invited one who I later came to know as Ken. Excitedly he introduced me as a travelling Englishman, though for a while I felt like a little green man from Mars. Mother and grandmother lived with Kenneth and nine other children in a shack which contained two double beds but little else. The contrast between this and Sheraton Hotel where I was staying was painful.

'May I move in with you for ten days?' I found myself saying after only an hour. 'I am here to study and I can't think of a better way than to move in with you. I'll pay you what I'm paying the hotel.'

Mrs Dobson laughed heartily, 'You don't want to stay here. We are poor folks from the mountains.' The children went wild with excitement when at last their mother gave in.

That night I sat down on the floor and shared what God had done in my life and at Mrs Dobson's request read some verses from the Bible.

'Can you help me with some homework?' quizzed Kenneth. 'I can't do math.'

We sat down together and to the boy's delight worked at the sums he had been set. I refused to give him any answers but guided him to understand simple concepts. Soon he was eager to go on to more as he found he was able to get the answers right. When we had almost finished the sums he fished around in his trouser pocket and pulled out a metallic object. Holding it in front of my nose he challenged, 'Do ya' know what that is?'

'Yes,' I said triumphantly. 'It's a key.'

'It's more than a key,' he chuckled. 'That's my pocket money. It fits the money box to the pay 'phone so I can just help myself.'

I told Ken how I too used to steal money but how Jesus Christ had forgiven me and given me a brand new life. Secretly I admired his ingenuity and cunning. Poverty had turned him into a thief but not, as yet, into a hardened criminal. His eyes glistened as I told him of my prison cell.

'Here, I want you to have this,' he said planting a kiss on my cheek and pressing the little silver key into my palm.

Later that night when all was quiet a boy's voice broke the silence and prayed to God. I lay amid a tangle of smelly bodies and cried.

I left America on the Cunard Liner the QE2 and had five days at sea to reflect upon my ten months' trek. I had stayed in the palatial homes of the rich and powerful and also in ghettos where five children sleep to a bed and rats run under the floorboards. I had seen over two hundred projects aimed at improving life for the poor and dispossessed. I had lunched with Senators in Washington, civil rights workers in Atlanta, hippies in Philadelphia, male prostitutes in New York and tycoons in Texas. Life would never again be the same and though my ministry has continued in Britain, the pull of America has been such that I have returned every year not only to preach but also to learn from a people who dare to grapple with the complex issues of a multi-racial, multi-cultural, hodge-podge of society.

When through the mists of Southampton Water I spotted the cranes of home I realised that God had given me a unique opportunity which would enhance my ability to minister more effectively in London.

9: Mr Vic and Sue

I was met at Southampton by John Troup, the treasurer of East Hill Baptist Church. He welcomed me home and assured me of the love waiting at Wandsworth for me.

'How's the house fund?' I enquired.

'We've got about £3,500,' he said. 'Not enough to buy a house in London.' I had accepted the call to the ministry knowing that the church could pay me very little and had no house for me to live in. I was willing to exercise faith for an income but a house was a major requirement. I could stay with the church secretary, a lady in her late 70's, for a time but that was no real solution. I had called the church to pray for a miracle.

'Wait till Saturday John. It'll come,' I said uneasily.

A welcome home party had been advertised so everybody with any connection to the church turned out. The eldest member was a man called Eber Kington, a retired baker, who was commissioned to voice the welcome and present me with a pulpit Bible. At the close of the evening he took me to one side of the church hall and said, 'Oh pastor! I have been praying for thirteen years for this church to have its own full-time minister.

Now my prayer has been answered so I am going to make a final donation to this work. I have given money to my children and made provision for my grandchildren. I am going to sell my house and move in with my daughter for the remainder of my days here on earth which may not be many. I have seen a house in Westover Road which will suit as a manse for many years to come. They want £7,500 for it and I am going to pay the balance.'

The miracle had come. I had a house to live in and my first pastorate had begun. During the first month of ministry I spent time tramping around the streets of my neighbourhood. Knocking on doors to introduce myself. Talking to kids on the common. As I came to the end of one busy day I wandered tiredly towards Westover Road. As I passed a parked lorry I noticed a man, not much older than myself, sitting in the cab.

'Hello,' I said. 'Got a job on tonight?'

'How the bloody hell did you know?' came an Irish voice through tightly clenched teeth. 'Oh it's only you Father,' he sighed with obvious relief as he spotted my collar. 'You must be Mr Vic. I've heard about you from the boys. You've done time I hear.'

'Yes,' I said, somewhat troubled that my reputation was limited to such a dubious distinction.

'You'll do well round here,' he assured me with an air of one who knew the ropes.

I was not quite so sure when the next week I made my first appearance at the youth club. Sullen eyes greeted my entry. The music was deliberately turned up full pelt. The door behind me slammed. I felt nervous but tried not to show it. Thankfully they decided to test me by a display of aggression towards each other and the doors rather than towards me. The tempo began to rise and I knew instinctively something had to be done to break the tension.

I walked deliberately to the record player and turned it off. 'Right, everybody sit! Wherever you are! Sit down!'

Angry eyes flashed. A group stood whispering in one corner. One cleaned his nails with a knife and looked menacingly at me.

'Sit,' I said staring straight at him. With a look of disdain he sank to his knees.

'Fair enough,' he scowled.

'OK. Everyone follow suit.'

One by one they sat on the wooden floor.

'I'll take that,' I said to Paul, holding out my hand for his knife. 'In future this hall is neutral ground. All weapons will be handed in to me at the door. Skinheads and Greasers have equal rights to this club. The first person to violate that rule will be the first to feel my fist. The two people who have broken the hinges on the back door can be down here in the morning to help me fix it. You root for me and I'll root for you. OK?'

They nodded their approval.

'Right, whose for British Bulldog?' I challenged.

One by one they got up and made their way to one end of the hall leaving me alone in the middle. 'Bulldog!' They charged. By the end of the game I was bruised and exhausted as one after another tested my strength.

The next morning the two boys who had broken the door met me and set about repairing the damage.

'I need two Yale locks boys. Will you go down to Cusdens and get a couple for me?' I gave them a pound and sent them packing. 'Get a receipt lads,' I called after them. Twenty minutes later they arrived back.

'Ere y'are guv,' said one handing me two boxes and a piece of paper. I checked the receipt.

'Hey this says one pound two and six. I only gave you a pound.'

'Oh, that's all right Mr Vic. We chipped in the rest.'

'Thanks,' I said looking with dismay at the receipt. 'Hey, this says "one" Yale lock not two.'

'Oh that's all right. They cost one pound two and six pence each. We nicked the other one for you.'

I was flabbergasted. These boys were on probation and had risked a sentence stealing to please me. A great step in building a relationship.

'Thanks lads,' I said with genuine gratitude. 'You don't mind if I go down to Cusdens and pay them do you?'

'What! You must be mad,' they protested; but still allowed themselves to become close friends in the weeks that followed.

A while later this friendship was put to the test.

A new youth came to the club. As soon as I saw him I knew there would be trouble. He had it written across his face.

'Hello. What's your name?' I asked.

'Jesus F. . . Christ.'

'Now come on. You know from this collar that that name is special to me so let's start again shall we. What's your name?'

'Jesus . . .ing Christ.'

Before I had time to think my fist had coiled and he lay at my feet. I looked round at a sea of startled faces expecting any second to be on the floor myself.

'Hey Mr Vic. You 'it 'im.' They turned and ran in to the club excitedly shouting my praises. With one punch I had become a hero.

As my first Christmas neared I wondered how to make the carol service meaningful for such an unruly bunch. Whenever they came to church it was with lighted cigarettes and transistor radios.

'Look fellas. I want you to help us put on a tea party for some pensioners and then take part in a nativity play.'

'You must be jokin' Vicar,' said Paul who had by now become spokesman for the inner circle.

'No I'm not! I'm going to tell you the story once and then you act it using your own words.'

On the day they fussed over the old folks, many of them proving to be real ladies and gentlemen under the hard exterior of alien clothing.

When the service began I bit my lips with

worry. Paul wandered out on to the platform with his arm around his latest chick. 'They don't look much like Mary and Joseph to me' I thought as they stopped centre stage.

The girl turned and whispered. Paul looked stunned.

'Well it weren't me luv,' he shouted in mock horror. The play had begun. Colin climbed the pulpit steps to portray John the Baptist.

'Right, look out you lot. 'E's comin' and you betta be ready!'

Even the most staid members of the church heralded it as a great success.

A young lady stood at my side and squeezed my hand with affection. I had first met Sue at a Baptist Missionary Society Summer School. I was not booked to attend Bexhill B, but I was preaching at the nearby St Leonards-on-Sea Anglican Church. After the service I was standing at the door saying goodbye to the worshippers when suddenly a group of young people came running up the steps. Unceremoniously I was thrown into the back of a van and driven off to Bexhill. Sue was a ringleader in this group. She had heard me preach at her home church in Enfield. I was impressed by her sparkle and prettiness so I asked her to go out with me but she said no because she was already dating another man.

A few months later I was speaking at an inner London conference on evangelism and spotted her in the audience. As I spoke I couldn't take my eyes off her. As soon as I had finished my address I made a beeline for my dreamgirl. I asked her to come out for coffee.

'No,' she said. 'I've promised to be back in Enfield within an hour.'

I was not sure whether I was being given the brush off or not so I persisted. 'Here's my address,' I said hastily pushing my card into her hand. 'Write to me.'

To my amazement a few days later a letter arrived. A date was quickly arranged and three weeks later we were engaged. We would have to wait eight months to get married so Sue came over to Wandsworth most weekends.

As we walked across Wandsworth Common a few days after our engagement we saw a large group of teenagers gathered in an excited mood.

'Come and see my Greasers,' I said to Sue with a chuckle. As we came closer it was plain that the excitement was a pre-fight warm up. One of their girls had been beaten up crossing the East Hill Estate.

Sue became the object of a temporary diversion and not a few wry jokes about dirty old vicars.

'We are going to do the Skins,' Paul threatened coldly.

'Just a moment Paul. You can't go into a fight with all these little nippers hanging on. I would advise you to send everyone under thirteen packing.'

This he did to the jeers of the skinny brave youngsters.

Sue clung nervously to my arm.

'Whose your vicar?' I asked the group.

'You are Mr Vic.'

'OK, then let me give you some advice. Some of you have never been in a real fight before. Sue and I have just made a pact with each other that in future we shall not make any major decisions without asking God to guide and help us. Now I realise you are not Christians but I think you should pray about this fight before you go charging off into battle.'

'Bow your heads,' rasped Colin. 'Go on Mr Vic. You pray.'

I did. When I opened my eyes, unbelieving eyes caught my glance.

'I don't feel like fighting any more,' said Colin sullenly. Gradually the group dispersed.

My associations with blacks in America had given me an insight into their culture and an ease of communication with them. I had been called a 'nigger' as a term of endearment by blacks and a 'nigger lover' by whites whose prejudice clouded their judgment. In Wandsworth I found a growing community of Jamaicans. One or two already attended the church on Sundays but it was a white establishment which tolerated 'coloured' people. I believed and so I preached equality in Christ and held out the hand of friendship to all, regardless of race or social status. One couple left the church and joined the Methodists in protest. Most others agreed with my basic philosophy so we soon had a joyful interaction of all God's people. Eric Davids, a Jamaican plumber's mate, was made a deacon because of his true spirituality and so the door was open for others to come in with expectations of meaningful ministry within the ranks of the church.

One day a huge bear-like black man attended the church. 'I want you to come round to my house and dedicate it to Christ,' he said as his enormous hand enveloped mine. I looked into his face. Though grim and somewhat pitted like the surface of a planet, his eyes were warm and gentle. Here was a natural brother. When he told me a few days later that he had seen the rum side of life I was not surprised.

'The Devil's been after me Pastor. I've not been a good man,' he said with sorrowful tone.

'Ah. The Devil's had a bit of a field day with my life too Pat,' I confessed openly. 'I'll tell you what. Why don't you and me join forces? Together with Christ we'll lick the Devil.'

The Patterson family became friends and members of the church. On one occasion a couple of years later when I had been through a rough day and felt the bottom had dropped out of my life, I went to a Bible Study at which Pat sat beside me. Though I was supposed to lead the study I had nothing to say. I was drained empty. I would not willingly admit my failure to the group. After all I was the pastor. I had a duty to appear spiritual. I turned to Psalm 119, the longest in the Bible, and began to read with the intention of going from verse 1 to the end. When I reached verse 25 my eyes became fixed to the words: 'My soul cleaves to the dust, Revive me according to Thy word.' I choked and stopped reading.

'That's just how I feel tonight,' I sighed heavily. 'I'm fed up. I'm earthbound and I need something to help me.'

'Kneel down Pastor,' boomed Pat as he stood towering above me. His great hand came down like a crushing weight upon my head as he began to pray the sweetest prayer of healing a man has ever received.

Sunday services began to be more relaxed as we became a growing family. Often they were uncomfortably unpredictable. On one occasion I was starting a service on the theme of the Christian family. Before my sermon I said to the congregation: 'Stand up and face each other where you are in the pews. Does anybody have a family problem which needs to be shared here this morning?'

As soon as people shared their trials and griefs spontaneous prayers broke out in little groups around the church as believer comforted believer. Tears flowed but so did grace.

Often sermons were interrupted by people asking questions. John Antrobus, a playwright, had become a Christian through Alcoholics Anonymous and started attending our church. A true non-conformist he set about challenging my sermons with at times lively exchanges between pulpit and pew.

Sue coped with this strange freewheeling ministry admirably. We were married in late

August 1970 and soon she was involved in her own special brand of service. We had decided that our home should be open to all callers regardless of status. What we did not know was that during the next four years 360 people would have been housed in our enormous six-bedroomed manse.

The largest number of visitors at any one time was only fifteen but every guest was a new challenge to our faith. Often we were literally penniless. On one such occasion we had three Americans to stay. They were part of a group of ministers and laymen from Alabama on a preaching tour of London.

'How can I feed them?' pleaded Sue. 'We've got no money and no food.'

'Just scrape together what you can darling and pray they're on a diet,' I quipped to avoid the seriousness of the situation.

I returned to the dining room where our guests were laughing and joking over breakfast. A few minutes later Sue popped her head around the door: 'Just going shopping love,' she said with a smile.

'She's gone mad,' I thought. 'How can she go shopping with no money?'

Suddenly Joe Lett jumped to his feet and ran after Sue who was about to leave the house. 'Give me that bag Sue. We three men are doing the shopping this morning. We want to have the experience of using our English money.' He grabbed the list from Sue's hand and disappeared. An hour later he not only returned laden with food but insisted that Sue take the change from his £10 note.

Kington House became a refuge for runaways, tramps, drifters, students, visitors from the USA, kids kicked out of their homes, and even girls brought from the local police station so that they needn't be locked up in the cells overnight. Whilst most of these were short term visitors who coped remarkably well with our lack of furniture, two became longer term members of our family.

Betty Milligan was a fine, hard-working single parent of four whose husband had deserted her some years previously. I visited her in hospital one day where she had been admitted for what we all thought was to be minor surgery.

'In confidence, Mr Jackopson, I give Mrs Milligan about six weeks to live,' said the surgeon bluntly.

Six weeks. She is only in her early forties. She has four children to care for. My mind raced back through the years of my childhood.

'She must be told,' I urged.

'Yes and you had better tell her,' came the reply. 'She knows you and she trusts you.'

My heart sank as I realised the awesome responsibility upon me. I could cope with a hundred rebellious teenagers but one dying woman was enough to send me into a flat panic.

'Pray for me,' I urged the young people who met at my house that night. 'I must tell Betty tomorrow morning so that preparations can be made for the children.'

As I entered the ward I stood at the end of the bed nearest the door. Betty looked up and smiled.

'I know what you are going to say Mr Vic, but I want you to tell me anyway. I'm dying aren't I?'

'Yes Betty you are dying but you are going to die to live.'

Over the next few weeks we arranged for her sister to look after the two younger daughters whilst Malcolm, who was almost twelve, and Marion, the eldest sister who was fourteen, would come to live with us at the manse. When Betty eventually died Sue was in hospital giving birth to our first daughter, Christy. Now we had a family ready-made. I began to appreciate what it meant for people like the Smeeths and the Weekes and the many others who had, from time to time, tried to cope with my unpredictable nature in their homes. Marion was a sweet-natured girl who became a great friend to Sue but Malcolm was as changeable as the wind. He was like me and to that extent I failed him as much as anyone had failed with me. Some told us we were fools to foster with such a young baby of our own and maybe they were half right, but we maintained our responsibility as best as we knew how until they were old enough to leave our nest.

The arrival of Christy was to allay for ever my sense of inadequacy in close relationships. I had been haunted by fears of marriage and fatherhood. Only days before our wedding I was ready to call it off. I loved Sue but thought I would make a poor husband and an even worse father. My own childhood had been such a nightmare that I didn't want to risk bringing children into the world. What would happen to them if I died? For at least two generations the Jackopson fathers had not lived beyond their mid-thirties. Would I leave orphans too and allow history to repeat itself?

I had come close to marriage once before but the girl's parents disapproved of an ex-convict coming into the family. Sue's parents had no such qualms.

'It's not what he has been but what he is,' they had told Sue.

I tried to let Sue down gently by telling her she was better off without me. As a pretty school teacher she would not have any difficulty finding a man who would be a better risk.

'I love you now but I'm afraid I shall not have enough love to give. If you want to know why I have had so many girl friends it's because I dare not allow anyone to get too close.'

She cried. I felt cruel.

'You silly man. Don't you realise I have enough love for the two of us? With the bovver boys you are tough, but with me you are kind and gentle. I'm not going to let you throw our happiness away just because you are scared.'

Now I held Christy in my arms. My daughter. God must have known how much love I needed because twenty months later, on Christmas Eve, Ruth Estelle was born. I now had three women in my life each of whom came as a special gift of love. We talk openly together about my past and share together the miracle of God's love and power to remould a life into happy fulfilment. Christ is at the heart of our home, and though I'm sure I make many mistakes as a father and husband, I am convinced the circle of fear and despair has been broken.

The church in Wandsworth grew. My understanding of ministry developed as I shared in the lives of a community in which all the skills of counselling and evangelism were stretched to the limit.

In 1974 it looked as though my task at East Hill was complete. I had no idea where God was leading me but I knew it was to new horizons of faith.

10: A New Vision

In June I told my deacons that I would be leaving Wandsworth in six months.

'Where are you going?' they asked.

'I have no idea but we must start praying now for a successor who will lead the church on. I am a builder, a pioneer, and I must be ready to move on.'

Many inside the church and outside cried openly as the bond of relationship moved on to a new dimension.

'We are not going to keep you minister,' said Pat looking doleful. 'I have been expecting this for some time and I know it's right but we love you and we don't want you to leave us. God's will be done.'

Days later I attended the annual speech day at Spurgeon's College. Who should I bump into but my old friends John and Myrtle Roche. John had interviewed me for church membership at Chatsworth almost fifteen years before but had now moved to a little village called Godstone. I told them of my decision to leave Wandsworth.

'What are you going to do?' asked John.

'Oh I'm not really sure. Some business men have been urging me to become an itinerant evangelist, but I'm not convinced that's what God wants me to do.'

'Some big church is bound to snatch you up,' said Myrtle.

'I don't really want a big church Myrtle. I'm not ready for that.'

'But you wouldn't go to a small church would you?'

'Yes,' I replied confidently not knowing what was behind the remark.

'Well, we are without a minister at Godstone but it's only a very small village work,' said John who was always very practical.

That night I drove out to Godstone. What a difference to Wandsworth. A village green with quaint little cottages clustered around it. A pond with ducks. Near to the church a large council housing estate and youngsters not so far removed from what I had left behind in London. I prayed that God would guide me, believing that if this were the place of his choosing I would receive a clear call from the church.

A few weeks later that call came loud and clear but at about the same time I received a card through the post.

Sir Cyril and Lady Black
request the pleasure of your
company at a tea reception
to be held at the St Ermin's Hotel
where the Rev David Bubbers
will introduce the subject of
Evangelism Explosion.

'Let's go,' said Sue excitedly. 'I just fancy a nice tea.'

We sat and listened. I believed deep down that there was nothing very new I could be taught about evangelism – least of all from the United States where I had seen some of the most bizarre and sub-Christian confidence tricks passed off as evangelism. Had we not tried every means imaginable at East Hill? Lay Institute for Evangelism with Campus Crusade, Coffee bar evangelism, grand choirs and rock bands, great preachers and personal work on the streets, dial-a-pastor for crisis counselling, camps, retreats, missions, Bible clubs and so on. We were exhausted in evangelism. To my surprise, however, the concept of Evangelism Explosion not only seemed a new approach to personal evangelism, it had a ring of truth about it. We heard how it had been tried in Northwood but even more impressive to me, in Corby. Northwood could be written off as the 'Gin and Jag belt' where almost anything would work without much effort (such was the degree of my inverted snobbery and prejudice) but Corby! A steel town! If something is working there it must be at the very least worth investigation.

'What we need', said Sir Cyril at the close of the meeting, 'is a person who can take these concepts of training and introduce them to the churches of Britain.'

As he spoke Frank Cooke turned in his seat and addressed me: 'That's you Vic. You are the man they need. Would you like me to give your name to Sir Cyril?'

Sue squeezed my hand. We were of one mind.

A week later I sat in Sir Cyril's office. We talked about the invitation I had received to become minister at Godstone.

'It's a bit like my first church,' I said. 'They have no manse, they can't afford to pay me a salary. They have been served admirably by lay pastors for the past twenty-five years but they need building up.'

'I'll tell you what I'll do,' said Sir Cyril after weighing up the pro's and con's. 'I will arrange for a mortgage on a house which the church can begin to buy as a manse. You must have somewhere to live. I will also arrange to have half your salary paid by a charitable trust if you will give half of your time to promoting Evangelism Explosion.'

The church were 'cock-a-hoop' at the news. In late October I was inducted to my second pastorate.

Barely had I settled into my new home before my first major problem arose. A member of the small congregation, an elderly lady called 'Burb' by everyone, sent a message to say that her husband had left her taking with him every item of furniture from their council home. Not a chair to sit on. Not a bed to lie on. I sat down at once and telephoned everyone I knew. Within twenty-

Planning for Tomorrow

Please send me details of your Estate Planning Service ☐

Name

Address

_____ Postcode _____

Telephone No _____ 258/07

I understand I may be contacted by letter or telephone.

Data Protection: Please note that we never make your name and address available to other organisations. Naturally we will tell you of other products and services relevant to you. If you would prefer not to receive this information tick this box. ☐

BUSINESS REPLY SERVICE
Licence No BS 6354

London Life Limited
100 Temple Street
Bristol
BS1 6YJ

or phone now
0272-276056

four hours the fellowship had refurnished her home. Burb was not the kind of person to keep quiet about such an event. Within hours the whole village knew and the doors to homes and hearts were opened by a simple deed of kindness.

A few days later there was a ring at my front door. A distraught young couple were ushered into my study.

'My dad is dying in hospital. Will you visit him? We are not Christians but we are afraid for him.' said the tearful woman who had been introduced as Diane.

When I arrived at the Mayday Hospital I found her father in a ward by himself. An oxygen mask covered his face and the ravages of cancer had left their unmistakable mark. As I walked towards his bed his sunken eyes opened in startled amazement. His skeleton-like hands grappled with the plastic mask which he wrenched from his face.

'You're an angel aren't you,' he whispered reverently.

I smiled. I had not very often been mistaken for a heavenly being.

'Yes I am,' I said. 'An angel is a messenger from God and I do have a message for you.' I had just finished learning a new and clearer way to tell the main message of the Bible to those who wanted to know about eternal life. Now God had given me somebody to tell.

'I've wanted to know about God all my life but

never found anyone who could tell me. Will you?' he pleaded. 'I know I'm dying but I'm not ready to meet God. I'm not good enough.'

'No you're not,' I said. 'In fact nobody is. The Bible tells us that it is by grace – by God's kindness – we are saved; it is the gift of God and not because of works which we have done. The wages of sin are death – that is what we deserve; but the free gift of God is eternal life.

'When you said you were not good enough you were right because God's pass-mark is absolute perfection and none of us are perfect. All are sinners including me. We all fall short of God's standard, and deserve punishment.

God, however, loves you and does not want to punish you. It is because of his justice alone that the penalty of death hangs over the guilty. But he has found a way for us to have life by bringing his love and his justice together.

Jesus, who came to earth 2,000 years ago, was God in the flesh. He lived a perfect life but died on a cross the death of a common criminal. Why? Because he was paying the penalty for you and me. He took the rap for us. He died in our place. Because he was God he rose from the dead three days later to show that he had purchased a place in heaven for us.

He offers us the gift of eternal life which we can receive by faith. That is by trusting him alone.'

'Do you mean all I have to do is to believe?' he whispered.

'Yes. If you believe you will repent of your sin and put your trust in him.'

'What do you mean repent?' he enquired.

'Well, imagine you are wanting to get somewhere in your car and as you travel along you see a road sign in front of you which says you are travelling in the wrong direction. In fact in the opposite direction. What would you do?'

'I'd turn around and go the right way.'

'Yes, and that is what repentance is. What I have just shared with you is a sort of signpost which says you have been going the wrong way or your own way. Repentance is doing a U turn by confessing your sin, trusting Christ to forgive you because of what he has done on the cross, and accepting him as Lord of your life.'

'I want to do that,' he said with tears filling his eyes. 'How can I do it?'

'If you really believe and want to repent why don't you just simply pray this prayer:

Heavenly Father,
I confess that I am a sinner.
I have done many things for which I am ashamed.
Please forgive me.
Thank you for sending your Son to pay the penalty for my sin by dying in my place on the cross.
Please give me your gift of eternal life
as I put my trust in you.
Please be my Lord.

I want to live for you from today.
Thank you Father. Amen.'

Ten days later I visited David and Diane to make arrangements for a funeral.

'What did you say to my dad, Vic?' said Di with an inquisitive appeal. 'He was so happy and changed.'

Some hours later both husband and wife knelt down to pray asking God to give them new life and Christ to be their Lord and Saviour.

So began a new dimension in evangelism. Clear unargumentative communication of what had changed my life.

11: Mother

When I was twenty I made contact with my mother. My elder brother Eddie was able to give me her address. She had become the manageress of the Abbeydale Golf Club in which her husband was the steward.

I travelled up to Sheffield unannounced. I knocked on the door and was confronted by a portly ruddy-faced gentleman.

'I'd like to see Mrs Jackopson,' I blurted in confusion.

He looked at me with suspicion.

'You mean Mrs Harding don't you?' he said indicating that she was now re-married with children, the youngest of whom was six.

'Who are you anyway?' he said.

'I'm her son,' I declared with new boldness.

His mouth dropped open.

'Her son. What's your name?'

'Victor.'

'Well I'm her husband and I've never heard of a Victor. You'd better come in.'

The meeting was traumatic. I was the second son to be produced 'out of the cupboard'. Michael had lived with them for a short time and now lived only a few miles away with his wife and baby. Doreen, my younger sister, had been accepted from the start because she was living with my mother, and Eddy was known because he lived with my mother's sisters in Southampton.

Mother turned out to be a well groomed lady in her fifties. We never talked about my childhood together. The subject was too painful for both of us. I sensed that her mind was crippled with guilt. Once she apologised for not taking care of me. I began to pray the relationship between us would be restored and that one day she too might become a Christian.

Over the years we saw little of each other and on the rare occasions we did meet our eyes never really met. Nearly fifteen years after our first meeting Mum was taken to hospital in Manchester to have a breast removed. It was there that God miraculously answered the prayer for our relationship to be made whole. Our eyes met. My hatred turned to love and her guilt was banished. At Christmas she and Bob came to live in our home at Godstone. Despite the painful burns mother nursed from the radium treatment we had a happy family reunion with my own children happy to have grandma around.

In January we went as a family to America for three months, leaving my mother behind and confident of a complete recovery. I was in Fort Lauderdale, Florida, completing the training which would equip me to become the British director of Evangelism Explosion.

We were having a whale of a time for although we had no money our air fare had been paid and a house had been provided rent free. The odd preaching engagement provided enough to live on so this was to be the adventure of a lifetime.

Our complacency was shattered when one day we got the news from my sister. 'Mum is in a coma. She has developed secondary cancer and is not expected to live.'

I became furious. Why had God let me down? Had I not prayed for years that my mother would become a Christian? Now separated by thousands of miles she was dying without Christ. I had always been too embarrassed to talk to her about the gospel for fear of losing the relationship. Now it was too late and God was to blame.

'There's no point you getting angry with God,' Sue soothed me. 'What you need to do is to go home and see her.'

'And how am I going to do that?' I bellowed. 'It will cost the top fare to get an immediate flight. About $800 round trip. Where do you suppose we are going to get that kind of money?'

'From the bank,' she said calmly.

I laughed caustically. 'And do you suppose, young lady, that the bank is going to give me a loan of $800 to get out of the country? Come on, it's the biggest con in the book. "Please Mr Bank Manager, my mother is dying and I want to get out of the country. Do you mind emptying your safe to help me?" No. This time we are really in a mess.'

Sue prevailed and nagged me all the way to the North Ridge Bank.

'You go in alone. I will stay in the car with the children and pray.'

'I'd like to see Mr Ralph Mittendorf,' I told the receptionist.

I was shown into a superb office where the friendly face of Mr Mittendorf greeted me. He won't be smiling in a minute, I thought to myself. Though he was a member at the Coral Ridge Church our acquaintance had been brief. He knew I was due to speak to the men of the church the following night.

'Mr Mittendorf,' I took a breath, 'I need a loan of $800 to return home to England where my mother is dangerously ill and not expected to live much longer.'

'What collateral do you have Vic?' he asked.

'None,' I replied honestly.

'What do you have at home?' he quizzed.

'I have even less there,' I said realising the comedy in this situation.

'You had better fill out these forms and let us see what we can do.'

I looked at the forms and wondered why Americans filled them 'out' whilst Englishmen filled them 'in' and yet achieved the same end.

Minutes later $800 stood on the desk in front of me.

'That's not a loan Victor. That is a gift from the Lord which I do not wish to see again. Before I came to work this morning I prayed that God would show me one person I could help. You are the answer to my prayer. Our men will be praying for you tomorrow night.'

I was speechless. I returned to the car where I sank into Sue's arms and cried.

When I arrived at the cottage on the outskirts of Morecambe where my mother and Bob had made their retirement, all the family were there with the exception of Michael who had many years before had to leave the country to avoid some of his criminal activity catching up with him.

'She's still in a coma,' said Doreen in hushed tones. 'She may not even realise you are here.'

I went upstairs. As I entered the bedroom my mother groaned, opened her eyes and whispered.

'Victor. I knew you would come home.'

I tried not to cry. I walked quietly over to the bed and kissed her.

'Mum. I want to tell you about Jesus and how he loves you and wants to give you eternal life. Will you listen to me?'

'Yes,' she nodded.

A few minutes later she was praying to receive eternal life and drifted back into the coma repeating, 'Jesus, I'm trusting you. I'm trusting you.'

Three days later she was dead. My family asked me to conduct the funeral at which I shared with them the message of Christ's power to make all things new.

I returned to America a happy man, knowing that the home we never shared together on earth would be more than compensated for by the place which Jesus has prepared in heaven.

Another event on that trip to America was to act as a turning point in my career.

For days I had been bothered by a pain in my throat. Not a sore throat. Something quite different. Sue urged me to see a doctor. I didn't want to go for fear of what it might cost. I had taken out insurance for her and the girls but had decided to save money on myself as I was normally healthy. When at last I gave in and reported to the doctor I was surprised to be told after a full examination. 'Reverend Jackopson, when you have dressed I would like to have a talk with you in my office.'

I nervously fumbled with my buttons as I did up my shirt wondering what was so serious that he had not told me straight out.

'You have a growth on your thyroid gland. I want you to take this letter along with you to clinic to get a scan and be ready in the morning to go into hospital and have it removed should it prove to be malignant.'

I sat in the car for an age. My mother had just died of cancer. My father had died of tuberculosis at exactly my age. At the very least I reasoned, if I have cancer of the throat my one ability will be seriously damaged, for it would mean an end to preaching. I tried not to tell Sue but it was no use, she knew me too well. I could not hide my fear from her.

The following morning I sat in the waiting

room waiting to be called by Dr Benanolti. Suppose he gives me six months to live, I worried, what would I do with my life then? I decided I would do nothing different. I would continue to be a minister preaching the word of God and I would also continue to teach ministers how to more effectively equip their members to share their faith sensitively, conversationally and effectively.

'You're OK,' smiled Dr Benanolti. 'The scan results were negative. You have what we call a clinical nodule which is unfortunately all too common among people such as you who use your voices for public speaking, especially those of you who wear restrictive collars. Give your voice a complete rest and go along to the ENT clinic for a course of drugs which will remove the cause of your trouble.'

I was almost sick with excitement and relief. Sue and the girls thought it great fun to have me under orders not to speak. I failed, however, to obey doctors orders. I had come face to face with the vulnerability of the body and the need to fulfil God's plan each precious day. As long as I have a voice or the power to communicate my life is dedicated to evangelism and equipping others through the church to fulfil their service and witness.

12: Evangelism Explosion

Godstone is one of those rare villages which seem to have the best of all worlds. Close to London with all its advantages and yet set in the midst of some of the most beautiful countryside of Surrey, nestling in at the foot of the North Downs. The old village atmosphere with its quaint ramshackle of cottages, pond and green within a stones throw of the M25 motorway. The 'would-be-rich' on the hill and the 'sometimes-poor' in the valley. Ancient parish church and modern chapel. Kaleidoscope of personalities and outstanding characters.

I think God must have known that my ministry there was going to be a short one – so much had to be crammed into the two years among the people of Godstone.

Evangelism Explosion was begining to grow. More and more churches saw the potential of ordinary Christians equipped to share their faith openly. Some churches were even beginning to expand with new members introduced to the faith because of the clear witness of those who had been taught.

When the board of Evangelism Explosion began to pray for a national director to establish a centre for the work, I was chosen. It was with some sorrow that I said goodbye to my dear friends in Godstone and with not a little fear that I accepted the challenge of returning to Southampton.

God had done some wonderful things in my life. I had been brought from a prison cell into the ministry of the church. My life had radically changed from irresponsible self-centred confusion to at least a desire to serve God and fulfil his plan for my life. I had left the town of my childhood with all its bad memories and associations behind. Could God really be calling me to turn again like some latter day Dick Whittington? I hated the idea and told God so. Sue was equally adamant. 'I'll go with you,' she said, 'if God has called you to Southampton – what else can I do? But I don't have to pretend I like the idea. I want to stay in Godstone.'

We moved!

Eight months later I went through a period painful even to write about. I had never been able to understand people who talked of breakdowns or depression. My whole experience of the Christian life was so overwhelmingly happy that the occasional down day was no more than a Monday morning blues which had vanished before midday. I lived up to my school boy nickname of Yo-yo – never-down-for-long. 'Things could be worse. Remember above every cloud the sun shines. It'll be another day tomorrow.' A thousand slogans of comfort, many of which I must have used before, were brought down on my head as I went through the dark, dark tunnel of depression. Sleeping pills and Valium became my constant companions. 'Why are you crying Daddy?' Christy would plead. I wanted no one. I felt that even my friends wanted my downfall and was sure that my days of ministry were over.

What was happening to me?
My mouth is dry.
I feel dull and long for death.
What do people think?
I don't care what people think.
They are out to get me.
I'll fight. I'll run. Oh damn it, I'll sleep.
Where are you God?
I can't pray.
Who sinned – them or me?
They want me tested.
They think I'm crazy.
I am crazy.
I've been working too hard.
I hate Southampton.
Why did you bring me back here God?
'Daddy, don't cry any more.'

Two or three months passed like a lifetime and eventually reason began to return. Sue, meanwhile, had not only taken over my job, which included running the office and acting as host to a choir of sixty Americans, but was also mother, nurse, comforter and spiritual counsellor. Her strength and gentleness led me back, at first reluctantly, to God.

The natural tendency seems, in my own experience at least, to be defensive about such personal pain. It is easy to blame others or circumstances or work or that most unquantifiable evil called pressure, but when faced with the truth most, if not all, of the blame comes to roost much closer to home in the mind, in the emotions and most of all in self accusation.

Serious questions had been posed during and immediately after the experience. Where, for instance, was God when I needed him most? I realise now with the perfect science of hindsight at my disposal that God was hidden by my unwillingness to see him. In the middle of my confusing depression I had felt alone, beyond my immediate family and the Billingtons (my doctor and his wife), but that was nothing to the isolation I felt during the following year as I began with God's help to rebuild my life. Could Christians really be so insensitive and even cruel? No. It was me feeling sorry for myself. In my wounded pride I had isolated myself from many who loved me. I had not trusted them. I resigned from my duties at the church and transferred to the safety of a larger congregation where I could hide in anonymity and lick my wounds.

One or two colleagues on the board of Evangelism Explosion had begun, understandably, to question whether I was still a suitable director for a nationwide organisation. The majority, however, were happy to see me released from pastoral duties for a while to concentrate my efforts into building what was rapidly becoming a major contribution to evangelism in Europe. I began to see a dream coming true as thousands were equipped to share openly their experience of Jesus Christ. The Reverend Edna Black, whose enthusiasm had stirred others to adopt Evangelism Explosion, became a strong friend whose confidence in me was like a transfusion of hope. My ministry was not at an end but a new beginning. Areas of my life not yet surrendered completely to the authority of Christ were to be repented of and submitted to his Lordship. The agony of depression was part of God's wonderful grace in showing me areas of personal weakness and inadequacy. It would be easy to blame an unhappy childhood but I needed to face myself honestly or deny the road to maturity. I could no longer live with excuses. God had been working patiently with me from the beginning, now I must choose between giving up or going on in his strength.

The next two years were marked by a personal change which I still find surprising. The war I had waged against myself was no longer important. I found absolute fulfilment in my family and work. Evangelism Explosion began to grow in a way beyond our expectations. Germany, Norway and Holland developed thriving EE ministries and ministers from other countries around the world came to training courses in England. God had performed a miracle by equipping me to teach as well as preach.

Often during this period my thoughts returned to Fort Lauderdale where I had faced the question of what God wanted to do with my life. I could not escape the realisation that only one half of the answer was being lived. In spite of the success of Evangelism Explosion I was no longer pastor of a church. I preached most Sundays in pulpits around the country but I had lost touch with people in my own town of Southampton.

In the winter of 1980 a single event happened to highlight my Fort Lauderdale decision. A choir was due to visit the city in July so I was busy searching for accommodation. I knocked at the door of a house in Bassett Crescent East.

'Hello. I'm the Reverend Jackopson. I believe you received a letter from me concerning an American choir from a Memphis Presbyterian Church and a youth group from Riverside Church in Atlanta.' My introduction had been well rehearsed and by now the response was almost predictable. 'Oh I'd love to but. . .'

Move on, I began to think. But no. There was something in the face of the man which made me stop.

'We are about to move house,' he continued.

'Where are you moving to?' I enquired.

'Oh we don't know yet. You see we have just lost our son Jamie. He died, so we want to get away from this house.'

'Jamie,' I thought to myself. Jamie was the

name of a little boy of six who had died during my first pastorate in Wandsworth. His mum and dad were close friends. I had spent four anxious days with them at the Atkinson Morley Hospital. I had helped them take the decision to donate Jamie's kidneys and to allow the life support machine to be switched off. I had conducted the funeral and had to explain to Christy where her friend had gone. I saw the same bewildered expression I had seen in the eyes of my friend Chris Briggs.

'Have you a faith to cope in a time like this?' I found myself saying.

'We go to church but it doesn't help'.

'Do you mind if I put you on my prayer list? I'd like to pray for you.'

He didn't mind so the next morning after my prayers I wrote a letter of comfort.

It was not until four or five months later that I received a call from the man's wife. 'My name is Norma Hayes. May I come and see you. I feel so depressed.' She then tearfully told me of Jamie's brain haemorrhage and subsequent death, as I tried to console her.

Jamie! Strangely, had little Jamie Briggs lived he would have been the same age as Jamie Hayes. I was reminded of a poem I had written when Norma went on to tell how her son had come in from a meeting one night to ask his daddy if he could have permission to be baptised.

'Do you understand the meaning of Baptism? Do you understand that it is a symbolic dedication of your life to God?'

'Yes, I understand that,' said the boy. 'I have made a decision for myself. I want to believe and I would like to be baptised on January 1st.' The baptism never took place. On December 19th Jamie was taken straight to heaven.

The Hayes became real friends. Eventually Jim, the boy's father, became a Christian himself. He and Norma started coming to church with my family but it was soon evident that God had an even greater plan in our meeting. 'You miss being a pastor,' he said one day as we travelled together. No one except Sue had noticed that. Deep down I knew that I would soon have to return to that other half of my ministry. The church we were attending was one of the finest churches in the country for its biblical teaching and drew many hundreds from miles around, but we were becoming more and more restless to engage in effective evangelism in our own part of town.

With the blessing of David Jackman and other friends at the Above Bar Church, Southampton, we set out on a new adventure. Notices had been placed in the *Saturday Evening Echo*, invitations sent to friends, and nervous prayers said again and again. Now the test. Who would come?

To our surprise over forty came that first Sunday to wish us well in the launch of Grace Baptist Church. It may only be in my spare time, thought I, but it feels so good to be back in pastoral charge of even an embryonic church.

The next Sunday, gone were the well-wishers from other churches; we were down to a congregation of nine. I determined to preach as though there were a thousand souls to be saved. In my mind's eye, I could see in every one of the hundreds of empty places, an eager searcher and potential member.

'You'll have to do something about the music,' counselled Sue. 'We need a piano.' She was absolutely right. I have never heard anything quite so pathetic as the attempted praise of that morning. The next day, via *Yellow Pages*, I found myself at Montague's piano salesroom in Fareham.

'What you need is a Knight. They have a lovely sound for community singing,' said the salesman.

'Good,' I returned, 'Knight it shall be. How much discount will you allow me?'

He offered 10 per cent.

'Fine. Now we only have one problem – that still leaves nearly £2,000 to pay and we have no money,' I smiled. 'We do want to buy the piano and you do want to sell it to us, so perhaps we could discuss how to overcome this temporary problem.'

'How about a twelve-month interest-free loan,' he suggested.

'Great, so long as we still get our 10 per cent discount,' I bargained.

The piano was delivered for the next Sunday. A dozen people had gathered and we sang ourselves dry with thankfulness. A few days later our good friends Bob and Ruth from Texas called to invite us out to dinner. We laughed together as I told them the saga of the piano. At the end of the meal Bob shook my hand. 'Oh, by the way, Vic, how would you like an early Christmas present? Ruth and I want to buy you and Sue that piano.'

Confirmation of our church planting came on the third Sunday.

'I usually go to another church,' said John, 'but I have come here this morning. By the way this is Danny.'

He went on to tell how on the previous day he had inadvertently bumped into Danny in the shopping precinct; though I suspect it was the other way about, and it was Danny who was rolling drunk and brutish, and bumped into him.

'Get out of my way or I'll thump your . . . head in,' Danny had cursed.

'You can't do that,' John, a somewhat puny graduate from Southampton University, had replied. 'You can only harm me if God allows you to and he's not going to allow you.'

This led to a conversation and an agreement to meet together the next morning to attend church.

'I couldn't take him to my church,' John told me later, 'people would stare at his clothes and tattoos and make him feel out of place, but I knew you would welcome him.'

So we did. Over the next three years we welcomed what can only be described as a grand mixture of humanity.

There were some, like Stanley and Jennifer Bute, who came by transfer from other churches but most came in as a result of direct evangelism.

There was David Lloyd, for example. He had been witnessed to by David Gibson, a fellow student.

'I've given him a copy of your book, *Hitch-hikers Guide to Heaven*. I think you should visit him,' urged the medical student.

I did. Dr R. T. Kendall of Westminster Chapel had come down to Southampton as part of his training in Evangelism Explosion.

'Well, R. T.,' I said, 'tonight we are going to visit the University halls of residence. There you will have the opportunity to share the Gospel with a first-year politics student.'

Some two hours later David Lloyd was in the Kingdom and a few weeks later he was baptised at a local swimming pool, where each month we baptised new members into the church.

Soon hordes of children from the local council-house estate swelled our Sunday school. The church was growing. The young, the old, the professionals, teachers, bankers, welfare workers, artisans and the unemployed.

How often I thanked God for the answer to a vision. Evangelism, caring, lively worship: all were happening within a growing church. The medical lecture hall was an ideal location for Sunday worship. Everything else would have to happen in homes but at least we would be inconvenienced for a purpose.

As I continued throughout these four years to serve Evangelism Explosion, the church could be only my spare-time occupation. I may be teaching in Liverpool or Plymouth or somewhere else but that did not matter too much. Stanley and Jennifer Bute had been sent as my right hand and left hand. So long as I could get home most weekends they and others would handle the mid-week teaching and various other crises of a new and vibrant young church.

In 1983, however, I was faced with a new dilemma. Alongside the growing church was the burgeoning ministry of Evangelism Explosion in

Britain and also in Europe. Folk from the Scandinavian countries, Germany and France had for some time past attended training courses in Britain. Now, as a natural and progressive expansion of the work, they demanded leadership, and I was invited by the International Board of Directors to assume the role of vice-president responsible for all of Europe between Iceland and Israel.

Between the church and these new and greater responsibilities I would be increasingly torn. The time had come for a full-time minister to become pastor of Grace Baptist Church.

Enthusiastically, I led the church to call a friend who had just come to the end of a course of study at the London Bible College. In November, Malcolm Deall was inducted as our Pastor. We had fond illusions as a family that I could stay on as an elder. This was, after all, our spiritual family.

One month later tragedy struck the home of Malcolm and Mary Deall. To lose a child of any age is an ordeal most parents cannot begin to contemplate, but to lose a child only weeks old by mysterious cot-death syndrome must be devastating beyond all imagination.

How could we understand? We couldn't. We could only offer comfort and love. The Butes were marvellous as usual. They had that wonderful knack of knowing just what to do in a crisis. Practical care and methodical efficiency blended with a Christ-like strong love.

Perhaps, in retrospect, we should have tried more to appreciate the psychology and depth of loss. If so we failed, for the relationship between Pastor and elders, instead of cementing, disintegrated. With heavy hearts we and the Bute family recognised that conflict between the leadership would damage the fragile flower of Grace. We must leave to allow God's choice pastor space to plough a different furrow. (The church is now part of the Southampton King's Fellowship.)

The timing of our heavenly Father is always perfect. What I could not have seen, he was already preparing. Evangelism Explosion had been an integral part of my life for more than a decade. It had been established in Britain and was spreading throughout Europe as a serious contribution to churches of all denominations in the equipping of ordinary Christians to share their faith. I believed in the concept and thoroughly enjoyed teaching via interpreters, and jet-setting the capitals of Europe; Prague, Paris, Copenhagen, Bonn, Geneva, Stockholm, Amsterdam. Surely I had arrived. Success. Position. Prestige. Pride and increasing arrogance. Warning signals were flashing. I had been promoted to my greatest level of uselessness, for I had become an executive when God's call upon my life was as an evangelist.

Whilst I had worked in the British Isles for the UK board I had considerable freedom to engage in evangelism. I could, in my spare time, plant a church or conduct missions. Such activities kept me in touch with ordinary, unpredictable humanity.

In Europe, on the contrary, I could do very little in the way of personal evangelism because of a language barrier. I accepted, therefore, more and more invitations to preach at missions and even at the occasional crusade. If necessary I could speak through an interpreter for these longer meetings.

The International Board of Directors in Fort Lauderdale wisely saw the conflict of interest. An invitation to conduct a crusade in Cape Town, South Africa, became the litmus test of my calling. Whilst I was over there at the beginning of 1985 an ultimatum came from the Head Office. No more missions. No more crusades.

Sir Cyril Black happened to be in Cape Town on one of his annual visits. It was Sir Cyril who had, several years earlier, introduced me to the work among the black churches throughout the region. I asked if I might talk the matter over with him.

He tapped his chair as he listened to my dilemma.

'Don't you think the Lord is telling you something in all of this, Vic?' he counselled. 'You have much experience as a pastor and as a teacher of evangelism, but you are first an evangelist. You must ask yourself the question whether God hasn't been preparing you to do the work of an evangelist. If that means moving from Evangelism Explosion, then that's the decision you must make.'

I knew instinctively that the old sage was right. Four months later I was back in his office receiving help and advice on how to set up what later became known as Hope Now Ministries, the vehicle which would enable me to continue both the teaching of evangelism and direct evangelism of all sorts.

13: Hope Now

New beginnings are a time for dreaming of the future and reflecting upon the past. He is a wise man who allows the lessons of experience to become the reins guiding and controlling the way ahead. Success and failure, arrogant pride and child-like vulnerability, daring enthusiasm and desperate insecurity were just some of the ingredients God revealed to me as I nervously inched towards establishing Hope Now Ministries. A recipe for disaster unless God could order from the chaos something good. He had begun a work in me, that much was evident, but the process must go on. 'If I am to bring hope into the lives of others', I mused, 'then I must be an example of hopefulness.'

Six months after leaving E.E., a group of more than a hundred supporters gathered at Westminster Central Hall for the launch of Hope Now Ministries. Dr R. T. Kendall charged me to take Philip the Evangelist as my model of ministry. He was available to be used by the Holy Spirit at immediate notice to speak to the great crowds of Samaria or to one lone traveller on his way from Jerusalem to Ethiopia.

Availability. Yes, that was the key. I would be available to churches and groups of churches, to individuals and societies. Soon invitations were coming in from all over Europe, the USA and

Africa but as far as possible I refrained from booking my diary more than six months ahead.

It was at the beginning of June 1985 that my availability would be put to the ultimate test. I was sitting in front of the television watching the *News at Ten*, when an item came on which made my blood boil.

For several days the police had been escorting a convoy of broken down buses and battered vans away from Stonehenge and through the country roads of Wiltshire and Dorset. The so called Peace Convoy of hippy travellers had attempted to set up a pop festival site on Salisbury Plain, much as they had for a number of years, to the disgust and dismay of local resident farmers. The previous year there had been a violent showdown between the police and the convoy in what became known as the 'Battle of the Beanfield'. Now, to my consternation the unkempt ne'er-do-wells had invaded holy ground, for the report showed them pouring in their hundreds to the New Forest.

I grumbled and complained at the sacrilege, that such a work-shy bunch of troublemakers should be allowed to disturb the beauty and tranquillity of the forest where decent folk liked to walk and rest.

'You're getting old and crotchety,' joked Sue. 'Don't you suppose there's another side to the story?' she challenged.

The next morning, whilst I was having a time of prayer and meditation, I felt convicted about my prejudice and anger, so I confessed it to the Lord. As I did so I was reminded of a verse of Scripture: 'If your enemy is hungry feed him; if he is thirsty, give him something to drink.' (Romans 12.20). This I did not want to hear, so I determined to cast it out of my mind. The more I tried to rid myself of the thought the more it impressed itself unrelentingly upon my mind.

I stopped praying and immersed myself into the Word of God. I was studying Proverbs chapter 25. There to my surprise and disgust were the very words I had so desperately attempted to avoid. 'If your enemy is hungry give him food to eat; if he is thirsty, give him water to drink.' (v.21)

'Sue,' I choked, 'we're going to have to feed this bunch of ne'er-do-wells.'

To my surprise, she agreed. Not that Sue is uncaring but she is very careful when it comes to spending money.

When we had finished stacking the boot of the car with food at Sainsburys, I drove off nervously to the New Forest. As I drove towards the site I was flagged down by one of the many men in blue. Thank goodness I had donned my dog collar. He waved me on through past the battery of press photographers, television crews and radio commentators. I drove to the far side of the site and started to unload the goodies.

Two children came running over to inspect me. They looked like images from a Dickensian novel. Eyeing me suspiciously one of them asked. 'Who are you mister?' I told him my name and suggested that he go and tell his mother that this food had fallen out of heaven. He needed no second invitation. Within minutes hungry hands were grabbing and sharing.

'Nice one,' smiled Fagin's double. 'Some of these kids haven't eaten for days. We've had to spend all our money on diesel being shunted from one place to another.'

'What ya do this for?' challenged one who would later be known to me as Looney.

'You'll never believe it,' I said, 'but I did this because I was angry with you.'

'H'm. I'd like to see what you'd do if you were a friend.'

I felt sure he would not understand but I felt compelled to tell him anyway. 'God told me to feed you,' I blurted out.

'Yea? Well we're all on a spiritual search too y'know.'

Soon I was sitting around one of the many campfires talking about Jesus. Most did not want to hear. Some listened politely. Others simply wanted to argue or to talk about Mother Earth and a plethora of strange metaphysical phenomena.

'You should talk to Phil,' nodded one whose eyes were in a fixed stare focused on the soot-blackened kettle perched precariously on the fire. 'He's into your Jesus.'

'Wanna cuppa?'

'No thanks,' I lied, eyeing the assortment of dirty mugs.

'Why do you do this?' I asked genuinely wanting to know the answer.

'Well, let me put it like this,' chirped the one with the dishevelled Mohican haircut. 'If you had a choice between this and a bed-sit in Brixton which would you choose?'

On my way back to Southampton I had much to contemplate. Sue was not at home so I guessed rightly that she was visiting Tim and Merrielle.

'Are you going back out to the forest to see them again?' inquired Tim after I had told them of the bizarre travellers.

I had not really intended to, but I could see that my friend was eager to see for himself. 'Let's go out this evening,' I ventured. 'Bring your bag with you. You never know there may be need of a doctor among so many.'

A bender is a makeshift tent; long poles are cut from trees, bent over and tied to form a frame, over a which a tarpaulin is draped. The sight of my doctor friend holding an impromptu surgery in one of these benders, with inquisitive patients crowding around the doorway to see how he worked, was delightfully comical.

'Just like Africa,' quipped Tim who had spent his early childhood years in Uganda among medical missionaries. 'Amazing. Everyone who came to see me needed a doctor.'

The next day a vet from our Bible study group joined me on site to check the health of the hundred or so dogs and cats. A newspaper had reported cruelty to the dogs, accusing the travellers of using them as footballs. 'Not so,' said Andy Sharp. 'You'd expect fleas and kennel cough with so many dogs in one place, but on the whole they are very well looked after.' I certainly never saw any evidence of cruelty. On the contrary, the animals were and are cared for sometimes better than the humans.

By the end of the week, 'The Mad Vicar', as I became known, was accepted as part of the furniture. The police soon recognised my car and would wave me through. The press and the media soon learned that I was not there for the benefit of their cameras. One television reporter became very angry when I refused to give my name, but I felt it was important to avoid any possibility of being misquoted and thereby losing all credibility with these social outcasts whom I was beginning to love.

Beneath the dirty exteriors were some delightfully sensitive people. These were all somebody's sons and daughters. True, a minority were bad but no more than in society generally. Most were naive Huckleberry Finns. Some had chosen the lifestyle to escape the materialism of what they called Babylon. Others simply preferred the companionship of like-minded drop-outs. Some were highly articulate and well educated but mixed with ease among the illiterate and those who, in former times, would have been locked up in state asylums. A society in microcosm, stripped of its status symbols, wearing the same dirt but travelling together as one family. Not quite the anarchistic enemies of the country some had branded them. 'Medieval brigands' they may be in the distant corridors of Westminster but on the turf of Stoney Cross they looked more like playful companions.

The confrontation between the forces of law and order and noisy playful anarchy came to a head on a Saturday night. The High Sheriff had posted notice of a court order for the eviction of the site. Behind the scenes elaborate plans were being drawn up for a police raid. Nervous huddles of frightened 'anarchists' sensed like rabbits that danger lurked nearby. A site meeting was convened and everyone spoke at once, no one listening to anyone else.

'They'll thrash us.'

'It's the Beanfield all over again.'

'They know they've got to kill us – it's the gas chamber.'

'We must stand.'

'We must run.'

'We must stay together. That's our strength.'

'Why pick on us. We're doing no harm.'

I turned to Tim Selwood, a non-stipendiary Anglican priest, who, like me, had been drawn into the fray. 'You know what they need Tim – a bridge. Someone who will act as a bridge between them and the authorities.'

Some around us heard our conversation and before I knew what was happening I was propelled to my feet on the back of a lorry to address the crowd.

I made my proposal to a hushed sea of wide-eyed hippies. One aggressively shouted me down. He was silenced by the others.

'This man's a friend,' I heard them protest.

Tim and I were given authority to go with two of their number to negotiate an orderly withdrawal.

At well past midnight we were still talking in the Chief Superintendent's office at Lyndhurst Police Station.

'I sympathise with you, Reverend. I know you are doing your best but it's the Forestry Commission you should be talking to, not me,' he concluded.

The next morning, before setting out for Tewkesbury where I was due to preach, in the more familiar world of Sycamore Chapel, I telephoned the head of the Forestry Commission, a fellow Baptist.

'Here's the plan.' I began to spell out the plan agreed among the travellers. 'You hold off the police. On Monday scrap dealers will be invited in to tow away all unroadworthy buses and vans. With the proceeds of those sales, all the remaining buses will be taxed and insured by ten o'clock on Tuesday morning so that the convoy can move on with no confrontation.'

'This is not a church meeting,' he countered, 'how can we be sure they will do as you say?' He thought for a moment. 'I'll tell you what,' he suggested, 'tell them to take down the pyramid tent where all the music is blasting out. If they do that this morning, I'll take it as a sign of good faith.'

I did not believe they would respond to such a demand. To dismantle the symbol of their festival would mean a complete climb-down. As I hadn't time to visit the site myself I telephoned Tim Selwood. He and his co-worker, Peter Gardner, went out to the site and to my amazement, when they called me back that evening, it was with the good news that the hippies had agreed to my request. The pyramid was down. We had an agreement. That night Sue and I knelt down to rejoice and give thanks for a peaceful solution.

The next day I turned on the radio to listen to the early morning news and to my despair heard the announcement that at four a.m. several hundred police had surrounded the Stoney Cross site and with military precision moved in and surprised the sleeping convoy.

When I eventually caught up with the travellers they were on foot. Their buses and vans had been impounded; their personal belongings confiscated;

their benders burned; their dignity however was still, miraculously, intact.

The police had invited them to go to a reception centre at Marchwood. Some did and were treated kindly to breakfast and given train tickets to any destination of their choice. Most, however, heard the term 'reception centre' and had visions of concentration camp. Penniless and dishevelled, having lost everything, the little they owned, they decided to walk to Glastonbury where the annual CND festival was about to happen.

Sue and I caught up with the dispossessed as they camped for the night in a friendly farmer's field. We delivered bundles of clothing and boxes of food hastily collected in Tewkesbury. 'Nice one, nice one,' they choroused.

'What kind of a day have you had?' asked Sue, anxious for an update on events.

'It's been great,' burbled Looney. 'I asked for a rainbow and do you know I've seen three rainbows. One was on a lorry, and two in the sky; a natural one and, would you believe it, a rainbow coloured plane.'

His attitude typified the mood of defiant optimism and cheerful camaraderie reflected in the faces of the fifty to seventy faces around the bonfire.

The next morning I decided to accompany them on their walk to Glastonbury. I drove my car, supplied with first-aid equipment from St John's Church, Wimborne, and for the next two days tended sore and blistered feet.

By the time we reached the festival site at Pilton, personal friendships had begun to form and gradually signs of acceptance percolated through the ritual banter. At the gates I called the tired hikers around me.

'You have come to know me and I have been privileged to know you,' I opened to a sea of smiling, curious faces. 'Now before you go into the festival, I'd like to give you each a copy of the New Testament, so that you may be introduced to my best friend.' For a few moments happy pandemonium broke lose as Bibles were enthusiastically grabbed and dozens of shaggy heads hugged and kissed me. Soon they were lost in an ocean of pop pilgrims descending into the valley of tents and thunderous music.

That's the last I'll see of them, I mused as I drove back to Southampton in the company of Mozart's Clarinet Concerto in A wafting from my cassette player. But God had other plans. The end was to be but the beginning.

One week later, several hundreds of travellers were on the move again with all the attendant paraphernalia of media hounds and marching army of police.

Buses and vans confiscated from Stoney Cross had been impounded at Nursling on the edge of my home town. The deadline for the vehicles to be repaired, made roadworthy, taxed and insured or suffer the fate of the scrap merchant's masher had been set for 31st July. Christian friends rallied to support. Douglas, a youthful arc welder from Lymington came every day to put his torch to work. Anonymous mechanics worked side by side with panicked travellers under the ever watchful but good humoured eye of the guardian police.

Clothes, food, money – all flooded in as a gesture of goodwill, so that we could minister more effectively to the growing number of temporary sites.

My task of bridge-building was made much easier with the increasing co-operation and understanding attitude of the local police matched by a deepening trust between the core of travellers and the Christian community. Soon I was able to negotiate timetables and orderly procedures for 'moving on'. Skips were hired so that convoy sites could be left clean and tidy. Minstead Lodge, a Christian community in the New Forest, headed by Tim Selwood and Peter Gardner, was opened as a place of refuge. A Lyndhurst farmer allowed a bus to 'park up' so that a mother could have her baby in peace. Other residents gave temporary facilities for parking up buses to avoid 'illegal parking'.

Throughout the following autumn, winter, and spring, Peter Gardner and I were to be found in regular contact with one particular segment of the travelling society. The rainbow village progressed from Canada Common to Salisbury and on via Landford to Wylie. It was there that we commenced regular Bible study in Phil and Jill's bus. Several had already become Christians whilst many others were still searching for a spiritual reality. I had long since learned to accept that rags on the outside did not necessarily mean dirt on the inside. The desire for inner peace and purity of conscience seemed, if anything, more real among these 'medieval brigands' than among the respectable 'upwardly mobile'.

142

By June the small band of travelling Christians were ready to become witnesses for Christ at Glastonbury. Some who had taken Bibles twelve months earlier were now back and ready to take Bibles to their travelling friends. 'Hash. Speed. Acid,' cried the drug vendors plying their deadly trade as openly as a market stallholder would persuade housewives to buy a cauliflower or tomatoes. Amid the noise, filth and plethora of insistent voices promoting every kind of dark practice, shone the testimony of changed lives. Two travellers were baptised in a cattle trough in the field of a neighbouring farm. So began one exciting and unexpected aspect of Hope Now Ministries.

I continue in this his work of evangelism whether among the travellers or in the City of London business centres, schools, universities or churches. I travel to many parts of the world as a teacher of evangelism. I conduct and speak at conferences especially those designed to reach and equip men. But in it all I never forget how God took a frightened little boy, a teenage rebel, a vacillating and unpredictable young man, and by patient love began the life-long process of reshaping, remoulding, remaking. There will, no doubt, be many more failures for him to forgive; many more adventures for me to live, but nothing, nothing in all the world, will compare to the joy of knowing and serving God.

Dear Christy and Ruth,
I began by writing to my father. One day I shall be gone to heaven but you will not be left wondering who your father was or what he was like. You know better

than any book can tell you. You have lived with me these years. You know the real me. Vulnerable, impetuous, always working as though today were the only day to live. You have seen me laugh much and cry little. A leader among men and yet needing the reassuring love of home and family. I cannot tell if I am strong or weak. I do not know, when others judge, whether they judge me good or ill. But this I do know. You are flesh of my flesh. Whatever life may bring for each of us our love is inseparable.

I cannot give you wealth. I would not. For it is deceptive and fickle. Fame and stardom are empty illusions. I would not wish you ease for it is unproductive and uncreative. I do not even wish you joy untouched by pain or gratitude as character will have no room for growth. Beauty you already have but one day it, too, will fade.

My darlings, what I wish for you is peace in a world of conflict. Grace when you are hurt as you must be one day. Compassion and mercy to all regardless of colour, status or religion. A generous spirit which gives instead of grasping and humility in greater measure than your father was ever able to attain. Confidence to face life and death as two sides of the same coin. Faith in God for all things and above all these, love, to give and receive. Love that is honourable, pure and durable.

God gave you both a wonderful mother, whose love has sustained me through some of life's darkest valleys. Always love her too. I love you for ever.

Your Daddy